BACK HOME WITH A VISION FOR A MISSION

Pastor Jonathan K. Yeboah

authorHOUSE®

AuthorHouse™ UK
1663 Liberty Drive
Bloomington, IN 47403 USA
www.authorhouse.co.uk
Phone: 0800.197.4150

Scripture quotations marked KJV are from the Holy Bible, King James Version
(Authorized Version). First published in 1611. Quoted from the KJV Classic
Reference Bible, Copyright © *1983 by The <u>Zondervan</u> Corporation.*

Scripture quotations marked NASB are taken from the New American
Standard Bible®, Copyright © *1960, 1962, 1963, 1968, 1971, 1972, 1973,*
1975, 1977, 1995 by <u>The Lockman Foundation</u>. Used by <u>permission</u>.

Published by AuthorHouse 02/23/2017

ISBN: 978-1-5246-6603-3 (sc)
ISBN: 978-1-5246-6601-9 (hc)
ISBN: 978-1-5246-6602-6 (e)

Print information available on the last page.

Any people depicted in stock imagery provided by Thinkstock are models,
and such images are being used for illustrative purposes only.
Certain stock imagery © *Thinkstock.*

This book is printed on acid-free paper.

CONTENTS

HE GAVE ME THE VISION AND A LIFE FULL OF MIRACLES
- BACK HOME WITH A VISION FOR A MISSION.

JOHN 20: 21 SO JESUS SAID TO THEM AGAIN, "PEACE
TO YOU! AS MY FATHER HAS SENT ME, I ALSO SEND YOU."
'BACK HOME WITH A MISSION'

FOREWORD

At a certain stage of my life I thought I needed a platform from where I could proclaim the goodness of the Lord to the whole World concerning my entire life, hence the publication of this Book "BACK HOME WITH A VISION FOR A MISSION".

It's a Book of testimony for what the Lord had done in the life of the author. Psalm 119:24" Your testimonies are also my delight, and my counsellors." In effect therefore any prospective reader of this book will see the awesomeness of God's goodness; His great Grace and His amazing love towards a boy born into a Christian home, who not only turned away from God he also became a prodigal son.

Though he forsook the Lord his God, and lived a sinful lifestyle in the days of his youth; yet the Lord showed mercy, and gave him a prophecy of hope through a man of God in those hopeless days of his life. It was not only the prophecy which I received, I also had an encounter with JESUS. YES I SAW JESUS FACE TO FACE, in one midnight just as narrated in this Book.

In the face of all these hard truth, I did not change my way of life yet the Lord God showed me His great Grace, unmerited mercy and His amazing Love. When I was lost He never forsook me, and when He found me He forgave me all. Then I started seeking the Lord with all my heart, when I had an encounter at one night with the Holy Spirit, in the later days of my life and that day was the turning point for my life.

As it's recorded in this book, many transformations took place in my life; as well as many testimonies, miracles, revelations, tries and tribulations were also experienced, but the Lord my God provided solutions and gave me victory in all. I sought for the Lord and when I found Him, He showed me great and mighty things in His Word through the Holy Spirit.

This is a man born into a poor home who could not advance his education because of poverty and how he had the opportunity to travel overseas was in itself a miracle. The first ever revelation I received was a prophecy by a Pastor of a Church concerning my journey to Great Britain in my life time. It was a prophecy I never believed in those days until the day it was fulfilled. One thing significant which needs mentioning was that at one time, it became necessary for all the town folk of Bunso my hometown, to choose between the Almighty God and a fetish god called Tegari which was performing miracles in those days. I was about 10 years old boy, and not only did I choose to worship the Lord my God, I also took to the street with my senior Sister to denounce Tegari as false god, as we preached Jesus as the only Saviour. The Tegari followers did not only threaten to harm us, they also warned that their god had power to arrest us spiritually. They waited and waited but nothing happened to us.

I believe, that time was the beginning of my destiny the Lord had ordained for me to live on this planet earth. Another thing worth mentioning is that my big brother visited me when I was working in the City, and told me to join him to the Central Region to see a fetish priest of a shrine for more power, and protection but I refused to go with him. Though I was lost in those days and gone out of the way of the Lord yet I had faith in Him. My life from there on has been full of many tribulations; yet miracles and great revelations also took place unto this day.

As recorded and narrated in this book, the Lord my God has been so gracious unto me; He showed me mercy, grace, and love, even at the time I did not deserve. Presently my age is even a testimony in itself; for all my age group and all those I taught at School look 10 to15 years older than I am. All people everywhere are amazed at hearing my date of birth.

It's all because of JESUS and having activated my faith as narrated in this Book, the Lord has healed me of all my diseases. Now it is not I who lives, but the Lord Jesus who lives in me. GALATIANS 2:20......"I live by faith in the Son of God, who loved me and gave Himself for me." All the ailments the Doctors have pronounced or diagnosed for my body have all been rejected by me, by faith in Christ JESUS. Again the Word of GOD says in Isaiah 53:5, "And by His stripes we are healed".

I am now free from all diseases and no infirmity has power over me, because my body is the temple of God. The Holy Spirit is my Senior Partner, and He lives in me. Psalm 103: 2-3" Bless the Lord, O my soul, and forget not all His benefits: Who forgives all your iniquities; who heals all your diseases."

My first ordeal as a kid was an attack with rheumatism which nearly deformed my legs, if my Mum had not fought the disease with herbal medicine. The rheumatic pain never left me during school age and after, but the Lord had mercy and healed me of the ailment. Also I had an infection of tuberculosis at school but the Lord healed me of that dangerous disease.

Since then I have had arthritis, heart pain, shoulder and back pain, but I am now healed of them all. Before this day I was diagnosed by the Doctors with high blood pressure, bowel cancer, prostate cancer, cataracts in both eyes; and other infirmities, but the Lord my God had mercy and healed me of them all. Matthew 8:17 "He himself took our infirmities; and bore our sicknesses." Romans 8:37-39 "Yet in all these things we are more than conquerors through Him who loved us. For I am persuaded that neither death nor life, nor angels nor principalities nor powers, nor things present nor things to come, nor height nor depth, nor any other created thing, shall be able to separate us from the love of God which is in Christ Jesus our LORD." God loves all His children and if He did for me He will surely do it for you. HE GAVE ME A VISION FOR A MISSION AND A LIFE FULL OF MIRACLES. I entreat you to read on. BACK HOME WITH A VISION FOR A MISSION.

PREFACE

My mum who introduced God to me as a child, always made sure I attended Church service, especially on Sundays; and I continued going to Church as a Christian until I completed the Middle School education and worked as a Pupil Teacher at the Presbyterian School for two years.

When I grew up as a youth and travelled in to the city, I forsook the way of the Lord, and led a carefree life. This way of life I chose to live without God cost me almost everything and nearly my life.

I WAS LIVING A LIFE WITHOUT GOD, BUT HE HAD COMPASSION ON ME AND GAVE ME GRACE. HE DID NOT GIVE UP ON ME; FOR WHEN I WAS LOST, HE FOUND ME AND GAVE ME A NEW LIFE.

ONE DAY IN 1990, I DECIDED TO READ THE BIBLE, AND THAT WAS THE TURNING POINT OF MY LIFE. FROM THAT DAY FORTH I CONTINUED READING THE BIBLE UNTIL I HAD READ THROUGH THE BOOKS OF GENESIS, DETRONOMY AND BEYOND. THE WORD OF GOD SAYS YOU SHALL KNOW THE TRUTH AND THE TRUTH SHALL SET YOU FREE, "JOHN 8.32" WHAT I FOUND WHEN I READ THE BIBLE TURNED MY LIFE AROUND.

ON ONE OCCASION I WAS READING THE SCRIPTURE, WHEN THE SPIRIT OF GOD SWEPT ALL OVER ME, AND I

HEARD A SMALL STILL VOICE SAYING," YOU WILL HAVE A BABY BOY AT YOUR OLD AGE, AND HE WILL BE CALLED SAMUEL", I RECEIVED THIS MESSAGE AFTER SEEING A SMALL BABY IN A BABY COT IN A VISION.

IT WAS THIS ENCOUNTER WITH THE LORD, WHICH PROMPTED ME TO SEEK THE LORD VIGEROUSLY THROUGH CONSISTENT PRAYER AND SERIOUS BIBLE READING. I PURSUED GOD WITH ALL MY HEART THROUGH PRAYER AND FASTING, VISITING VARIOUS PRAYER CAMPS IN THE COUNTRY TO WAIT UPON THE LORD FOR DAYS.

IT WAS THROUGH SUCH PERSUIT THAT I RECEIVED A MESSAGE FROM THE LORD TO GO BACK TO GHANA ON A MISSION WITH THE GOSPEL FOR SALVATION OF MY PEOPLE. "BACK HOME WITH A MISSION", IS A BOOK OF AUTOBIOGRAPHY WHICH PRESENTS A PICTURE OF MY ENTIRE LIFE, FROM CHILDHOOD TO THE TIME OF FULFILLING THE MISSION OF THE LORD AND UNTO THIS DAY.

WHILE IN GHANA FULFILLING GOD'S PURPOSE I ENCOUNTERED MANY PROBLEMS, AND WAS FACED WITH MANY SPIRITUAL BATTLES, BUT I TRUSTED IN THE LORD AND AS FAITHFUL AS OUR GOD IS HE PROVIDED SOLUTIONS TO ALL THOSE PROBLEMS. AS A RESULT I ENDED UP WITH GREAT VICTORIES, AND MANY GREAT TESTIMONIES WHICH I FEEL MUST BE SHARED WITH

ALL AND SUNDRY JUST FOR HIS GLORY, HENCE THE PUBLICATINON OF THIS BOOK. "BACK HOME WITH A VISION FOR A MISSION."

IN ALL THOSE TRIALS AND TRIBULATIONS, I DID NOT FEAR, FOR I KNEW THE LORD WAS WITH ME. ISAIAH 41:10 "FEAR NOT FOR I AM WITH YOU; BE NOT DISMAYED FOR I AM YOUR GOD. I WILL STRENGHTHEN YOU, YES I WILL HELP YOU, I WILL UPHOLD YOU WITH MY RIGHTEOUS RIGHT-HAND." Vs. 11 Says... BEHOLD, ALL THOSE WHO WERE INCENSED AGAINST YOU, SHALL BE ASHAMED AND DISGRACED. THEY SHALL BE AS NOTHING. AND THOSE WHO STRIVE WITH YOU SHALL PERISH."

THE SPIRITUAL BATTLE I ENCOUNTERED WHEN I STARTED MY MINISTRY FROM DAY ONE TO THIS DAY WAS NUMEROUS AND VERY FRIGHTENING BUT GOD GAVE ME VICTORY IN ALL AS NARATTED IN THIS BOOK.

THE GOSPEL VISION CHAPEL OF THE LIVING CHRIST MINISTRY WAS REGISTERED AS A CHARITABLE ORGANISATION, TODAY TRANSFORMING LIVES AND SAVING SOULS FOR CHRIST.

DEDICATION

THIS BOOK," BACK HOME WITH A MISSION" IS FIRSTLY DEDICATED TO MY LATE LOVING MUM WHO TRAINED ME AS A CHILD AND INTRODUCED GOD TO ME WHEN I WAS A KID. SHE WAS THE REASON OF MY SALVATION IN JESUS CHRIST TODAY, AND I AM SO INDEBTED TO HER. THIS BOOK IS THEREFORE DEDICATED TO HER MY LOVING MOTHER. IT IS ALSO DEDICATED TO MY LOVING SON, SAMUEL BORN IN NOV.2000. HIS BIRTH WAS THE RESULT OF THE VISION AND PROPHECY I RECEIVED WHEN I SET OUT WITH DEDICATION TO SEEK THE LORD AND TO READ THE BIBLE IN 1990, AS NARRATED IN THIS BOOK. THE PROPHECY WAS FULFILLED AND THE BABY BOY DANIEL WAS BORN EXACTLY TEN YEARS AFTER THE PROMISE. MY SON WAS BORN IN THE SAME YEAR I LEFT FOR GHANA ON THE MISSION.

ABOVE ALL, THIS BOOK IS FIRST AND FOREMOST DEDICATED TO THE LORD MY GOD, WHO IS JEHOVA SHALOM, JEHOVA NISSI, JEHOVA TSEKENU, JEHOVAH JIREH; WHO PROVIDED FOR ME FROM BIRTH, AND SAW ME THROUGH ALL THE TRIES AND TRIBULATIONS DURING

THE TIME OF MY MINISTRY IN GHANA UNTO THIS DAY. INDEED THIS BOOK OF TESTIMONY IS PUBLISHED PURPOSELY TO TELL ALL MEN HOW FAITHFUL, HOW GOOD AND AWESOME OUR GOD IS.

Acknowledgement

MANY PEOPLE HAVE CONTRIBUTED IN ONE WAY OR THE OTHER, CONSCIOUSLY OR UNCONSCIOUSLY TOWARDS THE PUBLICATION OF THIS BOOK. MOST OF THEM REMAIN BLISSFULLY IGNORANT ABOUT THE TIME OF PUBLISHING THIS BOOK. NEVERTHELESS I WOULD LIKE TO EXPRESS MY GRATITUDE TO THEM ALL.

I SHALL ALWAYS BE INDEBTED TO THE LATE REV. DR. PHILLIP PhD. WHO NOT ONLY INTRODUCED ME TO THE SALVATION OF THE LORD, HE ALSO ENCOURAGED ME TO ENROLL INTO A BIBLE COLLEGE OF WHICH HE WAS THE PRINCIPAL. WE HAD A LONG TIME CLOSE RELATIONSHIP AND HE NEVER STOPPED ENCOURAGING ME TO WRITE A BOOK ABOUT MY EXPERIENCE AND KNOWLEDGE OF LIFE. HE USED TO MAKE THOSE REMARKS MOSTLY WHENEVER HE RECEIVED A NOTE OR A LETTER FROM ME. MAY HIS SOUL REST IN PEACE IN THE LORD.

ALSO, MY VERY SPECIAL THANKS GO TO MY SPECIAL FRIEND DANNY A TURKISH, WHO LIVED WITH ME IN THE SAME HOUSE. HE WAS LIKE A SON TO ME AND HE CALLED ME DADDY. HE IS A MECHANICAL ENGINEER

AND I.T. SPECIALIST, WHO HAD A GOOD KNOWLEDGE OF THE INTERNET AND THE USE OF THE COMPUTER.

HE HELPED ME TO BUY THE RIGHT LAPTOP FROM THE SHOP AND TAUGHT ME HOW TO USE THE P.C. FOR THE PUBLICATION OF MY BOOK. THE KNOWLEDGE I ACQUIRED USING THE P. C., MADE IT EASIER TO COMPILE MY BOOK. I OWE DANNY A GREAT DEAL OF GRATITUDE FOR ALL HIS HELP AND ENCOURAGEMENT.

WHILE THANKING ALL THOSE WHO CONTRIBUTED TOWARDS THIS BOOK, I MUST ALSO INCLUDE PASTOR BILL, THE SENIOR PASTOR OF PLAISTOW CHURCH, WHO WAS GENEROUS TO READ THROUGH THE FIRST DRAFT OF THE MANUSCRIPT AND GAVE SOME USEFUL COMMENTS. I OWE HIM MY SINCERE GRATITUDE.

FURTHERMORE, MY SINCERE GRATITUDE GOES TO ELDER BENSON, A GREAT FRIEND OF LATE AND GOD SENT BROTHER WHOM I MET, IN THE VERY TIME AND MOMENT I NEEDED HIM MOST TO HELP COMPILE THE MANUSCRIPT AND THE PICTURES OF THE PROJECT IN TO THE COMPUTER FOR ONWARD TRANSMITTION TO THE PUBLISHERS. MY SINCERE THANKS AND GOD'S BLESSINGS TO HIM AND ALL. ABOVE ALL I MUST GIVE THE LORD MY GOD ALL THE GLORY, FOR WITHOUT HIM THERE WOULD HAVE BEEN NO MISSION TO WRITE ABOUT. THE MISSION TO GHANA FOR THE SALVATION OF SOULS FOR

THE LORD WAS PROMPTED BY THE HOLY SPIRIT, AND WITHOUT HIS PROTECTION MY JOURNEY BACK HOME ON THE MISSION WOULD HAVE BEEN FUTILE.

I BELIEVE THE LORD WHO SAW ME THROUGH, WOULD WANT ME TO WRITE ALL ABOUT MY MISSION TO GHANA AS A TESTIMONY FOR ALL AND SUNDRY TO READ AND KNOW THAT OUR GOD IS GOOD and FAITHFUL, AND HIS LOVE ENDURETH FOREVER UNTO ALL THAT BELIEVE. TO HIM BE ALL THE GLORY.

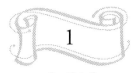

1

A PLACE I WAS BORN AND GREW

I was born and grew up at Bunso, a town in the Eastern Region of Ghana in West Africa. I was the eighth child of my Mum, who had thirteen children. My father was a peasant farmer and so was my Mum. My father had a second wife with other four children.

I was about four years old when I started to go to school with about forty children in class one. I was the first child of my Mum to be sent to school. All the children beginners of the school, were compelled and motivated to study very hard by our teacher, and those who did well, were promoted to a higher class before the appointed year.

When I finished the junior School in our town, I was sent to the Middle School at the capital of the Eastern Region. While I was at School my father passed away at home; and as a result, my Mum found it very difficult to look after me at school. She had to borrow from friends and relatives to buy my books, and my uniform and even to give me money for food was hard to come-by.

However, she did all she could to cater for me through my Middle School education. When I completed Form Four Middle School in the Eastern Region of Ghana, I could not continue my education because my Mum was a peasant farmer, and she could not afford to cater for my secondary education.

2

UNLIKELY PREACHER

I became a pupil teacher at the Primary School in my home town Bunso for one year and I was transferred to Asiakwa Presbyterian Junior School, to teach for another year. Asiakwa was the District Headquarters of the Presbyterian Church, and the seat of the Senior Church Priest.

Every Pupil Teacher was given additional assignment by the Priest to either lead the morning devotion or preach at the morning service of the congregation for one week in rotation. It was a big task for me, but the Priest made sure the morning Devotion was carried out properly, under his supervision.

In the course of my teaching work at Asiakwa, I decided to go for training to become a Clergy, but I failed the Clergy exam and I left the teaching field to go to Accra, the capital City to look for a job.

AN UNLIKELY
MESSENGER OF GOD.

My father was a Christian and a member of the Methodist Church congregation; but it was my Mum who introduced Christ to me at the Presbyterian Church, and she made sure I was always at the Church service especially on Sundays. I loved my Mum very dearly and I did all I could to demonstrate my appreciation for all that she had done for me before she passed away. May her soul rest in perfect peace.

When I travelled overseas I made sure to send all her needs that were dear to her heart. In-effect I asked her to send me a list of all her requirements she cherished most, and I made sure to supply her all.

My Mum was so honoured when she received the package containing her personal effects so dear to her heart which included Gold Plated Bedstead with gorgeous mattress; valuable Air Tight Box containing six full pieces of best clothes, sandals and shoes for old ladies, mosquito nets, some best blankets and beautiful bed spreads, including some money for her upkeep, sent to her from Britain by her son.

Just like a miracle the shipper, a Ghanaian who happened to know my Mum personally, offered to ship the goods to my Mum free of charge. The shipper explained that before he came to Britain, he was once a pupil teacher at our town and my Mum was his caterer for two years free of charge.

The news about the package containing my Mum's presents which arrived from London spread all over the Community, and it was talk of the town for months, even years. Also the news about the description of the contents of my mum's personal effects shipped to her from London, travelled to the neighbouring towns where some of our distant relations and friends live.

Most of them travelled a distance from those towns to see for themselves my Mum's presents from London. The idea that My Mum's presents were shipped from London, alone made it a sensational news.

She sent a message of her heartfelt thanks to me and added that the presents she received from me were all she needed before the time of her death. She added that she was greatly honoured for receiving her presents from me from London.

I was still in Great Britain when my Mum sadly passed away. In those days I was living a life without JESUS whom my Mum introduced to me in my childhood. I was lost at the time my Mum passed away, but I know now that my beloved Mum was always praying for me before she died.

She knew her Lord she introduced to me would never give up on me nor forsake me, but would save me at His own appointed time. Though I was lost yet I have some faith in the Lord. When it was time the Lord did not only save me, He also sent me to be His messenger. THE UNLIKELY MESSENGER OF GOD.

4

MY EARLY DAYS IN ACCRA

When I resigned from the teaching field, I bade my Mum farewell and I travelled to Accra in the capital to look for a job. In Accra I lodged with my half- brother called Edward who was working at the Ghana Harbour as a clerk.

Before I could find a job, Edward my half- brother asked me to quit from his rented room, because his girlfriend wanted to live with him.

I was saved from sleeping in the street by a woman called Maafio the Land Lady who allowed me to sleep in her pantry where she used to keep her big "kenky" cooking pots. Before then I had shown some kindness to her baby daughter, and that rendered me her favour in times of need.

Eventually, by God's grace, I secured a job as a messenger a few weeks later at the ACCRA Printing Press. The ACCRA Press was the publisher of the propaganda News Paper campaigning for Ghana's Independence.

At last Ghana secured Independence two years after my employment, and a number of the staff at the ACCRA Printing Press including myself, were transferred to Ghana PRINTING Press CORPORATION, a new Corporation which printed the National Newspaper called National Times.

At this time I was doing some correspondence Course in English and Accounts from Overseas, England; and the knowledge I had acquired in Accounts gave me the opportunity to work in the Accounts Department at the GHANA PRINTING PRESS Corporation.

5
MY GENERAL LIFE IN ACCRA

While at Mamprobi, I met a beautiful girl called MAGARET BENSON who was a student at a Commercial College. She was also a member of Ghana Christian Church and she invited me one day to a Church service. We became close friends, but then she noticed that the leader of the Church called "Prophet" was also interested in her. He never stopped pestering her and as a result she quit the Church.

In all those years in Accra, I was not going to Church regularly even though I was a Church goer in my home town. Originally I was born in to Presbyterian Church, and as recorded in the previous chapter, my Mum made sure I was at Church Service always, and when I grew up, I was though a church goer I was not a dedicated Christian.

When I travelled from home, I stopped going to church and I led a care free life. As time went by, Margaret and I became close friends, we got engaged and a year later we were married. We had two sons and the elder son called Daniel sadly died from high fever at the age of six.

A few years later my wife and I had an argument and she went to stay with her Mum for a long time and she would not come back. I followed up to her home town with my senior brother to bring her back but she would not return.

Consequently the marriage was dissolved. I moved on in life and I had a great time in those days working as an Accounts officer in that renowned Organisation, the GHANA PRINTING PRESS CORPORATION, which produced the leading national News Papers—The NATIONAL Times, GHANA EVENING NEWS and the GHANA SUNDAY MIRROR.

My boss, the Accountant was a British citizen called Michael who recommended a motor Cycle for me as a means of transport for the sake of my job. It was a great honour in those days for a youth of my age to own any type of transport or had a means of transportation. I had a good time with my motor bike.

Some years passed by and my Mum arranged for me to marry a girl called JUDY from our home town. The family then arranged for my would-be wife to visit me in Accra. She came and spent some few months with me, and in the course of her visit I found out that she was too lazy to do anything in the house even to cook. She conceived and brought forth a baby boy, called Seth, but the relationship did not work.

I lived for a long time as a bachelor, without a wife, until I met a girl also called MILLICENT. We became friends for some time and we got married in two years prior to my departure to Britain. We had one baby boy named William.

When I looked back I realised that my life style was totally un-Christ like, yet I had a measure of faith in Christ. I was lost, but when He found me He forgave me all.

PART TWO

MY FIRST DIVINE ENCOUNTER
IN MY EARLY AGE

In all these years I was studying very hard preparing for the Common Entrance Examination for my G. C. E. 'O' Level. I had enrolled as a part time student at the Extra Mural College of Ghana set up by the Government for the Workers who could not had the opportunity to enter University.

I was still enjoying my life as a single man, unattached, doing everything I loved to do, including learning, except going to Church. All I used to do was to attend a Church service once or twice a year mostly on Christmas day or on New Year's Eve.

The life I used to live was not in consistent with a Christian life, yet I trusted in the Lord. I remember one day in 1969 my senior brother called Joseph visited me in Accra and invited me to join him to see a fetish priest of a god in the Eastern Region for more power and protection. God forbid! I replied. I said to him, far from me that I would go to any other god for help. That's not for me; May God forbid, I added.

Even though I was not going to Church as I would have liked to, as a believer, I still had faith in the Lord. I give God all the Glory for He never gave up on me and never accounted my weaknesses against me but had mercy on me.

I learned very hard as I prepared towards the pending examination. Some few days prior to the exams, I was desperate to pass, so it dawned on me to fast and pray; and so I did. I fasted and prayed for three days from Friday to Sunday for sure success in the G.C.E. exams which was to take place the following week.

Then I had an encounter with the Lord on the third day night of my prayer and fasting; and it was awesome.

7

VISION OF BRIGHT LIGHT BALL

On Sunday night being the last day of my fasting, I prayed after reading my Bible and went to bed before midnight. I placed the Bible under my pillow, switched off the light, and as I laid on my bed less than three minutes – I saw a small BRIGHT LIGHT BALL- rising from under my pillow towards the ceiling.

I became perplexed but was curious to see exactly what it was. I followed closely every second of the event that was taking place; for my eyes were wide opened. The ball of light began to rise up towards the ceiling, and as it did so, it became bigger and brighter.

Before it got to the ceiling it had become a very big ball of light, shinning the whole room like a hundred fluorescent light bulbs put together. The light was as bright as snow but the atmosphere was cool and peaceful. This brilliant ball of light had this time rolled to the centre of the ceiling and stopped near my bed. Then it began to descend.

8

FACE TO FACE WITH JESUS

As it was descending the big ball of light began to reveal an image of a Man, tall, handsome cool and calm, shining like a morning star, dressed in a pure white shinning gown, long to the feet and stood right in front of my bed. He had beautiful bright eyes and as He looked intently at me, I KNEW IN MY SPIRIT THERE AND THEN THAT HE WAS JESUS.

The whole room was full of His Glory, and His presence illuminating a glow of light radiating brilliantly on all the walls as white as snow. The atmosphere was cool and so peaceful. I was convinced that the peaceful atmosphere experienced that hour could not be found anywhere on this planet earth.

There was at once some un-speak-able joy in my heart for having had an encounter with JESUS. Now I became curious as what He was going to tell me. I was desperate to hear from the Lord what He had for me; but He never spoke.

I laid on my bed motionless gazing at Him, muttering the name JESUS, JESUS, JESUS, all the time with joy in my heart. He stood calm in His full Glory, shinning like a star gazing at me in a loving and compassionate mood.

Having waited for some time without Him saying anything to me, I decided to touch Him myself instead. But just as I lifted myself half way from the bed and stretched forth my hands to embrace Him, then suddenly He lifted up His right hand and made a sign not to touch Him. I withdrew quickly; petrified, lying on my bed motionless.

Then all of a sudden, the man I called Jesus lifted himself up towards the ceiling and as He did, He turned slowly in to a big ball of light illuminating bright light in the whole room. Then this big ball of light drifted towards one corner at the far end of the room and began to disappear through the wall, and as He did the whole light in the room followed Him slowly through the wall; and entirely disappeared with Him.

The room eventually turned total darkness. I was left alone lying on my bed in the darkness, meditating hard as never before about all that had just happened.

In those days just as I've recorded in the previous chapter, I was though a believer I could not claim to be a dedicated Christian. So I kept asking myself, why me; why me; and if He was Jesus, why He never talked to me; so I laid alone in bed meditating on all these things for hours.

In fact it was a moment I would always remember for as long as I live.

9

SIGNIFICANT DREAM AFTER NIGHT OF VISION.

In the course of my long meditation, I fell asleep eventually and I dreamed. There were many people seeking entry through a secured gate leading to a secluded area. But only few were allowed to enter with a pass.

When I got there I was given a ring attached with a small green leaf as a VIP Pass to enter the gate. I put the ring on my finger and I was led in to a class room with children supposed to be taught, but when I got there, it turned out to be preaching a sermon.

As I preached I saw open heaven through the ceiling with someone descending from the sky in a cloud. I became very happy, and as I was shouting with joy some people came in from outside to see, and as I shouted the more with jubilation my eyes opened. I could not comprehend what actually happened, but now I believe God wanted me to be a preacher of the gospel.

10

UNMERRITED FAVOUR AFTER VISION

I was living at the Beautiful Estates in Accra East at the time I had a divine encounter with Jesus. In the following morning after the encounter, I went to Makola market at Accra Centre to buy fruits and vegetables as that was the staple food I wanted to eat after fast.

At the market something miraculous happened. All the sellers from whom I bought the fruits and vegetables would not accept payment from me for their products. I was stunned when the first seller gave the items, melon and oranges to me free of charge; but I was more petrified and shocked when the four other sellers from whom I bought the fruits and the vegetables refused to accept payment from me. To avoid more embarrassing situation, I rushed home from the market immediately. It was simply a miracle. All the fruits and the vegetables I bought at the market were given me freely without accepting payment. Yes, it was a divine favour indeed. Furthermore, I passed the G.C.E "O" Level with credit by His Grace. Glory be unto His Holy name.

THE DAY OF PROPHECY
IN 1968

Despite everything and the vision I had a couple of years previously I wouldn't either go to Church or live a consistent Christian life.

However, in 1968 on Christmas Eve, I decided to attend a big Revival Meeting of a Spiritual Church at James Town Railways Warehouse where the meeting was taking place. When I got there I saw a great crowd of people who could not gain entry in to the Church Service at the Warehouse building.

Somehow as if by miracle, I managed to go inside the building of the Church Service. It was indeed a big warehouse full of worshippers. The man of God was preaching when I got in, and many people were standing at the back of the congregation without seats, but I managed a seat somehow, as a lady offered me half of her seat. In less than an hour, the Man of God started ministering to some people as they were invited to the pulpit and prayed for.

Suddenly, the Man of God shouted for the ushers to bring a man, God had blessed, from behind the congregation. The Ushers rushed through the big crowd of congregation and touched many people but he said it was none of them. Eventually the ushers got to our seat and one of them touched me; then the Man of God shouted, "that's him let him rise up." I began to shiver for I was a very shy person.

Then the unexpected happened.—The Man of God began to prophesy concerning my life. "The Lord has blessed you", he said. "You are destined to go to Britain, Overseas. You will be like King Solomon, and you will be rich," Thus says the Lord." He concluded. That day I went home with mixed feelings. To be honest I did not clearly understand the whole episode; and I did not believe what he said either. Firstly, in those days it was not possible for a poor man's son to go to Britain or Overseas. Secondly I did not know anything about King Solomon at that time and who he was in the Bible. I simply decided to forget about it all, put all behind me and move on with my life.

THE SECOND PROPHECY
RECEIVED IN 1969

It was another Christmas Eve in 1969, and like any other occasion, many people attended various functions, and so I did. Even though I was not a regular Church goer in those days, I chose to attend a Charismatic Church Service in a School Building at Accra East. I enjoyed the praise and worship service very much and the sermon as well. Before the Church service came to an end, the Pastor called me to the pulpit, and started ministering to me. The Man of God prophesied to me saying "The Hand of the Lord is upon you. You are blessed; you will go to Overseas Britain, and you will be great." Thus says the Lord, he concluded. The Church Service ended after midnight and I walked back home, because it was a walking distance from the Church. I began to meditate about the message I had received from the Man of God as I walked home.

Then suddenly I remembered the similar message of prophecy I had received from a Man of God the same time last year. From that day on wards I never ceased meditating about the two messages I had received from the two Men of God on different occasions. The fact that, the two Men of God giving almost similar messages concerning my destiny on different occasions, astounded me indeed. The whole episode seemed to me as an anecdote, trying very hard to understand how possible all that I was hearing could ever be, seeing I had no means to travel abroad, neither had I any one to cater for me. I kept asking myself almost every day, how could this be, how possible could this ever be?

Little did I know that even though I had no one, yet God was there for me, and what He has promised He was also able to fulfil.

PART THREE

13

FIRST TIME BUYER

After the encounter and the Revelation I had in my room, and the prophecy received from the two men of God, I meditated upon all these things for many months and even years, but then I put all behind me and carried on in life as usual. I never decided to go to Church neither did I live a Christian life.

One day a Landlady of our house neighbour called Madam Josephine wanted me to be a caretaker in her other house at Kaneshie. She said she liked me because I was a boy of good character; she had noticed my good behaviour since I came to live in that house of her neighbour. She wanted me to live in her other house at Kaneshie with other tenants; and to be the caretaker of her property. Consequently, I moved in to the house and lived there as a caretaker for a period of time.

In few years later I bought my own property for the first time at Western Estates. These Estate Houses were built by the Government, after Ghana's Independence, for the workers who could afford their own homes. I was one of the first buyers and was happy to help my other two friends Brown Osei and Victoria to buy their own homes.

When I moved in to my new Home, I called it "Blessed Home of the Lord." I planted in my back garden, onions, tomatoes, cabbages, lettuce and pepper. I harvested more vegetables from my garden and sold to my customers at the Ministries, for extra income. In all those days I worked hard and learned very hard.

FIRST TIME HOME BUYER

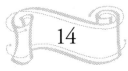

14

THE FAITHFULNESS OF GOD

I was completely ignorant about the ability of God. Little did I know that what God has said or promised, He was also able to accomplish it, as it is written in Romans 4.21'…' "'…what He had promised He was also able to perform."

Days and months passed by, even years yet I could not come to terms with what I had heard from the two Men of God. Somehow, whether by destiny or by miracle, I decided to attend Church Services, and also Christian meetings from there on.

It was one of such meetings at a Charismatic Church Service on one Sunday at Kaneshie- Winneba Road, in 1970, when the Pastor made an altar call for those who wanted to travel abroad to come forward. I rushed forward with others and the Pastor prayed for us all, one after the other. I was convinced after the prayer that God is truly faithful, for I believed, it could be possible for me to go overseas as the other two men of God had prophesied.

15

YEARS OF HARD WORK AND LEARNING

In all those years I was still an employee of the GHANA PRINTING Corporation, popularly known as GHANA PRESS CORPORATION. I was also doing a part time work, buying and selling in my spare time especially at weekends. I used to buy ladies and gents clothes from Lebanese shops and sold them to my customers in their homes.

Also I ordered the latest fashion shoes "at that time" from U.S.A. for my customers as well. I did all that mostly in the weekends on my motor bike. Besides I grew more vegetables in the compound of my new home and sold to the public. I continued working at the GHANA PRINTING Corporation for about twelve years.

In the year 1970, the company offered voluntary redundancy to all interested staff; and I took the opportunity firstly, to acquire an extra income and also to leave the GHANA PRINTING Corporation for good.

16

Voluntary Redundancy
and Aftermath.

After the redundancy, I joined the NATIONAL PRESS, one of the communication machinery of the Government in 1971, as an Accounting Machine Operator.

Long before this time I had enrolled as a part-time student at the Extra Mural College where I studied English Language, Maths, Commerce, Accounts and Economics. I attended classes on week days after work from 6pm to 8pm, and often continued my studies at the Central Library until 10pm before I went home.

This exercise of part time studies at the College and at the Central Library till 10 p.m. continued for almost four years. In addition to all that, I used to grow onions and vegetables in my back garden as mentioned in the previous chapter, and sold them at the Ministries. I did all that mostly in the weekends. This was the busy way of life I used to live for many years until I did my G.C.E. "A" Level exams in 1972, but at the Examination Room, I collapsed after writing the English paper. I was rushed to the Hospital and it was revealed that I had over worked my brain and therefore the Doctor warned me to refrain from reading for a long time to come. Consequently, I could not write all the exam papers and therefore could not succeed in the G. C. E 'A' Level exams.

17

PROPHECY IN 1968 & IN 1969 FULFILLED IN 1976

I continued working at the NATIONAL PRESS in the Accounts Department until 1976. It was just like a miracle, when the door for me to travel abroad was opened to me in 1976 through a Cousin of mine I had not seen since our childhood. Truly God makes a way where there seems to be no way.

My Cousin called BENSON came from U.K. on holiday, and when I talked to him he agreed to invite me to Britain if only I could pay for my flight. As a result I secured my visa for six months visit to U.K. from the British Embassy.

I sold all my belongings to enable me buy my flight ticket, and in the month of July 1976, I travelled to the United Kingdom. What God told me through His servants in 1968 and 1969 was fulfilled in 1976. Even so in the face of all the miracle, whether by ignorance or spiritual blindness I failed to recognise what the Lord had done for my life. It was until, some few years later I got to realise, my journey to Britain from my home land was not by accident; it was a divine assignment. I did not know then, but I know now. Unto God be all the Glory!

PART FOUR

18

MY JOURNEY TO BRITAIN

When I secured my flight ticket, I went back home Bunso to say goodbye to my Mum. She was sad that I was leaving her but also she was happy that her son was going to Overseas and she prayed for me.

The night prior to my departure to U. K., I invited a few friends for a drink over coke and soft drinks, for I was a teetotaller, at the Ambassador Hotel, and bade them farewell.

The first time I flew in an aeroplane was during my journey to Britain. The flight was so sensational and it was the greatest experience I've ever had in my life at the time.

My flight to Britain was in the month of July 1976. And when we touched down at the London Heathrow Airport there was a great sunshine. Just like a miracle the sunshine continued the warmth well in to the month of October. Many Londoners testified and said the weather trend was very unusual.

19

MY LIFE IN BRITAIN

My cousin BENSON received me into his home at ILFORD until November, 1976. However my cousin BEN, under the influence of his wife asked me to leave their home after six months stay with them.

Quietly, I left their home to lodge with a friend called Bill and his wife at Balham in South London. They had only one room to themselves, and therefore had no choice but to leave their house in three days' time to lodge at the LONDON STUDENTS HOSTEL in South West London.

While at the Hostel, I received an unwelcome news that my former employers in Ghana, the NATIONAL PRESS, could not send my back pay to me in Britain which could have enabled me enrol in to a College. I was shattered at the unfortunate news, but I encouraged myself and set out to look for a job. I secured a job as a Chamber maid working with a number of girls in a Hotel. The Manager of the Hotel, who was a Greek liked me very much commenting among other good things about me, and said my spoken English was grammatically good.

I worked at the Hotel for a couple of weeks; and I got an Agency job at a factory where soft drinks were produced. I was put on a night shift and I worked five nights a week.

20

MY PERMANENT EMPLOYMENT AND PROMOTION

I transferred my accommodation from London Students Hostel to Southwest Students Hostel. While there I had another job at the LONDON RANK COMPANY, a renowned Organisation in Southwest London. I was offered a job as an attendant at the Receiving Bay on probation.

I worked very hard at the Receiving Bay and that earned me a confirmation as a permanent staff; and then a promotion of a transfer in to the Linen Room, a sub division of the House Keeping Department. I needed to work hard to secure a place in that renowned Company. It was a moment of opportunity I needed to seize; for I needed to save some money for my education in the college.

We were twelve staff in our department but I was identified as the most hard-working staff in the Linen Room. Besides I was the only staff who could prepare the Linen Room daily report in the absence of the Supervisor, for my knowledge of Book Keeping and Accounts gave me the advantage.

Eventually I was promoted as the Assistant Supervisor in my fifth year. I was also presented with a Long Service Award on my fifth year and so were many others. In course of time our Supervisor took ill, and she was admitted at the Hospital. I was offered the position as the supervisor in the Linen Room with eleven staff under me. All my staff were white men except one. They made my work very difficult for me, but I showed maturity and dealt with any unreasonable behaviour effectively.

In effect my boss appreciated my efficiency and considering also my Accounting knowledge, gave me the opportunity to be promoted as the Head of the Linen Department in few years later. At this time my employers had secured a National Insurance Number for me and that gave me an opportunity to work in Britain without much problem. I eventually ended up working at the LONDON RANK COMPANY for twenty years.

21

Further Education Was My Priority

Having secured a job, I needed a partner to help, if I had to continue my education in U.K. I therefore decided to arrange for MILLICENT my baby's mother in Ghana to join me. In effect therefore I sent a message for my senior brother to obtain a visa for MILLICENT to join me in Britain; but sadly it was not possible because she had been impregnated by another man.

I was so shattered when I received the message but there was nothing much I could do. Though I was desperate to continue my education but my income was not enough to sustain me enrol into a college.

PART FIVE

22

My Relationship

My first relationship in London was with a girl called MIRIAM an office clerk who lived at Lime House. It was a short encounter, and I only saw her occasionally. In the first six months I saw her only once and I did not see her again until I met a girl near my work place called MARGARET from Northern Island.

She was a student and she also worked part time in a nearby Hotel. We became friends and we were very much close. One Sunday MIRIAM paid me a surprise visit and met MARGARET with me in my room. She became jealous and was so angry that she refused even to sit down. She left the Room sobbing and she even refused me to see her off. I did not see her again for a long time after this incident.

My relationship with Margaret had become stronger and when we were found together in my room at the Southwest Students Hostel, I was asked to leave because friends were not allowed to stay overnight.

I found a single room accommodation at Harrington Gardens nearby. I lived there together with Margaret my girlfriend for a few months, and our relationship grew stronger and stronger. The only intuition of Margaret was to marry me, but I was not ready to go in to marriage at the time; for my only desire was to go to College, and Maggie a student herself could not support me.

Around this time my Landlord had decided to eject me for the reason that the single room was not meant for couples. As a result I looked everywhere for new accommodation and I secured a single room self- contained at Balham in South London.

My friend Margaret was determined to move in with me, but as I explained to her that it was not possible, she became furious. A bit of an argument was ensued between us, and she became so angry that she began to smash everything breakable in the room. The degree of her temper scared me out of the room and I disappeared from the scene completely.

Eventually, I managed after sometime to remove my belongings from the room and I left very hurriedly. I have never again seen Margaret since. In all these years I had forgotten all what the Lord had done for my life; who had opened the door for me and led me in to this country Britain. I think I was only being naive and ignorant as how to seek the Lord.

This Book is written purposely to tell all and sundry how God is good to me, even while I was still a sinner He loved me, and so He loves all who have faith in Him. Romans 5. 8"But God demonstrates His own love towards us that while we were still sinners, Christ died for us."

23

SURPRISE COME BACK
OF MIRIAM

One day I was at work when I received a telephone message from the House Keeping Office that a lady wanted to see me at the reception. It was Miriam who had surprisingly come back to see me. We talked about a number of issues, and I apologised for what happened on the day of her last visit at the Kensington Students Hostel. She invited me to her new found Council flat accommodation at LIMEHOUSE in East London. I visited her the following week and she asked me to share the three bedroom flat with her.

My First Marriage In Britain

I decided to move in with Miriam and as time went by she asked me to marry her. Well, I considered marriage when Miriam asked, for MILLICENT, my son's mother I left behind in Ghana could not join me because she got pregnant with another man.

Eventually Miriam and I got married and our wedding took place at West Ham Methodist Church.

25

OUR BIZARRE WEDDING CEREMONY

On our Wedding Day, my wife appointed her best friend called Susie to be the master of ceremony for the occasion, and asked her to make sure every guest was served properly and that all must have enough to eat. Many people attended the Wedding ceremony, young and old and they all enjoyed themselves very well.

Just as the ceremony advanced in to the late hour, my wife found out that plenty of the food she prepared for the Wedding was left over unserved. My wife, the bride fuming with anger left the head table rushed to the kitchen, swearing and cursing at Susie. A heated argument ensued between them as all the bemused guests looked on with amazement.

I went home that day embarrassed, ashamed and confused. Thus our marriage journey had started this day with hope and uncertainty. The unknown problem which was her bad temper emerged on the very day of our wedding. Her anger on that day never subsided until hours later, even into the following day. I realised that the degree of her temper was her biggest problem and it could serve as an obstacle in our marriage journey.

Both of us worked very hard in to the late hour of the day. I had two other part time jobs apart from my main work and my wife had three other jobs in addition to her main office work.

26

MY MARRIAGE LIFE

I used to get home an hour earlier and made sure her food was ready before she arrived. I was always in trouble if her meal was not ready at the time she came home. Also, it was worrying when I realised I could not even share ideas with my wife. Every discussion turned in to heated argument, anger and sometimes insults.

We could not even spend weekend peacefully together without heated argument. My wife hated to see me happy, the reason I did not know. The only one thing I knew was that her brother did not approve of our marriage.

Since I was the Supervisor at work, I used the opportunity to change my work rota to be off on week days instead of weekends so as to avoid my wife at home. Our life at home was like a cat and a mouse, it was not worth living.

The worst thing happened when I caught my wife and a man locked up in a room, when I returned home earlier from work on one Sunday afternoon. I held the man by his shirt and made an attempt to call the Police; but my wife supporting her friend helped him to flee, and this experience never stopped hunting me. She warned and promised to testify against me if I made it a Police case.

27

MY ILL HEALTH

I was very unhappy man indeed in my marriage journey. My health began to deteriorate and I developed heart pain for some time. My family Doctor referred me to the London Hospital for examination and treatment. The Doctors could not find the immediate cause of my heart condition, but the pain never got better.

My health problem continued to deteriorate for well over one year until one day the Doctors invited me to a meeting at the hospital.

When I attended the appointment, I met three Specialists around a table. They interviewed me from 9am to 12noon; and after they had returned from lunch they continued the interview until 3.p.m.

When the meeting was over they gave me another appointment to return to the Hospital in three days' time for the outcome of the interview. The Specialists concluded that my heart pain was the outcome of my domestic problems. They advised that the earlier I did something about it the better it would be for my health.

In effect therefore I decided with haste to quit my matrimonial home without delay and without notice.

28

MY NEW ACCOMODATION

Eventually, I found an accommodation at Queen's Lane in North London. It was a small "6 by 10" room which I called mini chamber. It could not even contain a bed, but that did not deter me.

Besides the house was very untidy and the carpets on the stairs and the landing were very dirty. Indeed it was terrible, but in all, I slept very sound in the first night like a baby.

In the following morning my wife showed up at the place of my part time work at dawn, wailing and crying aloud echoing the whole big building saying; if I did not want her; I should take Hagar "our maid "away with me, for she wouldn't like to die and leave our maid alone in the house.

I did not give much attention to all that she was saying, I just finished my job quickly and left for my main work. About two months later she sent a bunch of flowers to me at work through the florist.

I lived at my new accommodation in peace for the past ten months, then out of blues my wife showed up one evening. At this time I had transformed the place into a decent home and all the old carpets changed in to new. This pleased the Landlord and he gave me a bigger room to show his appreciation.

When Miriam came to see me that evening she was in tears. She came with an apology and asked if I could forgive her and take her back. She promised to be a good wife henceforth. At this time my general health was very splendid and my heart pain had completely disappeared. I was then a very happy man living in my paradise. My new found life was blossoming and therefore the plea of Miriam to take her back and return to the matrimonial home was totally ignored.

However, she never rested her oars, but consistently appealed through some notable elderly men, but all was to no avail. My wife's effort to get me back took well over two years, but not until she had promised through some elderly men not only to be a good and faithful wife but also to show love and respect at all times.

OUR RECONCILLIATION

Our reconciliation took place at a meeting organised by some notable elders who stood in as witnesses.

Before then I had explained to the elders all about my past ordeal, and how I nearly lost my life for the reason of bad marriage. They were in great sympathy and therefore promised to do all they could to make sure it did not happen again.

30

Back To Our Matrimonial Home & A Disappointing Marriage

Eventually, I returned to our matrimonial home somewhere in January 1985. Miriam made sure to pick me up in her own car from North London to LIME HOUSE in East London, on the day I returned. That day was Saturday, and her brother called Tony had arrived with his friend from Ghana and were living with her.

Then something miraculous happened in the very night of the day I returned to my wife.

That Saturday evening we celebrated the occasion before retiring to bed. Then after midnight, we woke up from sleep by a rattling sound of water to realise the whole flat was flooded to our kneel level. We rushed out in fear in our night dresses from the eighth floor to the ground floor.

We quickly went to the public telephone to contact the Security Agencies and the Charitable Organisations for help. They quickly rushed to our aid and we were given a new accommodation the following morning by the Council. We learned later that the big water tank which served the whole block of flats was seated at the top of our flat had a burst, hence the flooding.

We moved in to our new allocation immediately and this time my name was added to the Council Letting list. My brother in law and his friend who were living with us till the day of the flooding, moved in to our new home together with us. He was not happy that my name was added to the Council Letting List; but there was nothing much he could do about it.

My wife did her best to be a good and responsible wife but her brother caused a lot of disruption and confusion with his bad and wicked advice. He was also the contributing factor for the immense problem and confusion of our marriage.

After sometime had elapsed, it came to light, and it was common knowledge that there was a set plan either spiritually or otherwise to get rid of me after I returned to my wife. It became obvious that it was the Lord who rescued me from their plot of the untimely flooding on the very night I arrived.

The revelation knowledge received long after the incident had it that my brother in law who detested the marriage, had a plan to destroy me with a concoction prepared from Ghana; but it was a miraculous intervention by the Lord to save my life. My brother-in-law and others meant it for evil but God turned it round for good. The new house we were allocated, eventually became my property in the long run. In those days, even though I had forsaken the ways of the Lord, He never forsook me. His love for me and for all His children endure for ever.

31

OUR MARRIAGE ON
ROCKS AGAIN

In less than two years the marriage was on rocks again. There was an occasion for my wife's birthday party and many friends were invited.

The party was in progress and while I was serving and talking to some of our guests, my wife came in to the hall from the kitchen enraged. She complained bitterly that she had called from the kitchen several times as she needed help but I did not respond. When I told her, I did not hear her call, she told me I was lying.

Nonsense, I replied, do not call me a liar, I warned. She became boisterous, rained insults and slapped me in the presence of all our guests.

Are you mad, I screamed at her! Then she made another attempt to slap me again, but I gripped her hand firmly and I wouldn't let go.

She bit my hand and I gave her a big knock on her forehead with the other hand. The blow made her forehead swell up, and she run to report me at the Police Station. I followed up with some of our quests to the Police Station and when the Officer saw my bleeding hand, he asked, "who had done this to you?" After my explanation, the police found out that my wife was in the wrong.

They detained my wife while they gave me a letter to the hospital. The party ended unceremoniously and all our guests went away confused. From that moment onwards there had been no peace until the day of our divorce.

32

OUR DIVORCE AND AFTERMATH

I divorced my wife for the reason of adultery, but she refused to sign the divorce papers unless the adulterous charge was removed. She also indicated she would not remove her name from the Council allocation papers without which I could not possibly buy the property on my own.

Then I thought of an idea, subscribed by my Solicitor, to invite her for a meeting to see if we could strike out a deal. In effect, we had a meeting at a Restaurant where she agreed to remove her name from the Council allocation documents on condition that I dropped the adulterous charge from the divorce papers.

So we did, and our marriage was at last over, when the Decree Nisei and Absolute were received in 1986.

Before my wife left, she made a weird but a profound statement-"Joe "she said, "Indeed you have a strong spirit." She lamented. I did not know what she meant then, but I think I know now. She moved in to a house I had helped her to buy, and I also bought the Council Property for myself.

PART SIX

33

THE LORD HAD PITY ON ME.

One significant thing worth mentioning was that in all those years even though I had forsaken the Lord my God, He had pity on me and saw me through those hard times. I also believe very well that the Lord allowed me to go through all those hardship of life and of the marriage problems so that I may be pruned for His purpose.

Until the time of my divorce I had gone through hell in life as a youth for the reason of my disobedience. Thank God, all my life sufferings ended when I met Jesus and took Him as my personal saviour soon after my divorce. Having met the Lord through Bible reading and my personal encounter in one night, I made a decision to quit the bad life and my sinful behaviour as I began to submit unto the Lord.

IT WAS A GREAT TURNING POINT OF MY LIFE. I feared God greatly when I read the Bible, the word of God from Genesis to Exodus and beyond-

34

MY WEIRD DREAM IN 1989 ---- (A DREAM OF FRIGHT)

I was journeying to an unknown place in a dream, and I walked along a footpath in a field of vast area, like a farmland without human habitation. The land extended a distance away without an end, and I could see no trees on that vast land, except one standing afar, far away ahead of me.

I walked for about half an hour and before I could get near the tree, I lifted my head to see a figure standing under the canopy of the tree. I observed a bonny-skeleton man in tattered clothes, bushy hair and a very dirty figure as I approached closer. He was standing right in the middle of the foot path under the canopy of the tree; and I knew he was insane, and therefore was scared to pass him by.

I approached him cautiously and as I came closer, I observed that the dirty lean figure of a man standing under the tree was myself. I was suddenly gripped with fright, and was so petrified that I shook vigorously in bed and my eyes opened. I was still shaking in bed when suddenly I heard a voice saying, unless you stopped your bad way of life, you will surely be like him. When I heard the voice I laid still in bed with fright meditating over and over again the whole night of what I had seen and heard.

From that very day, I decided to stop my bad way of life and seek Jesus.

35

A Property Bought In 1988

Barely two years after our divorce, I applied for a mortgage from the Bank to buy my home. I became a Home owner till it became necessary for me to go back to my country, Ghana on a Mission.

IT WAS IN THIS MY HUMBLE HOME I SET OUT TO SEEK THE LORD WITH ALL MY HEART AND WITH ALL MY SOUL AND I FOUND HIM. "Jeremiah 28:13; and you will seek me and find me, when you search for me with all your heart."

36

THE TIME OF TRANSFORMATION MY FIRST TIME BIBLE READING IN 1989

After the divorce, I concentrated on my work and all went on well with me. I found a Good News Bible at my work place, and I decided to read it. IT WAS A TIME OF TRANSFORMATION.

When I read the books of Genesis and Exodus, the Word of God had great impact on me. Therefore I continued to read the Bible vigorously unabated. The more I read the Bible the more the Word of God became life to me. Instantly, and as the time went by I felt totally transformed.

I made more time to read the Scripture during lunch hour. I used to send all my staff for lunch while I stayed back to read. Sometimes I missed my lunch for the sake of reading the Bible. It was through this process of reading the Bible, when one day in 1990, I had a VISION.

VISION OF A BABY IN 1990

I was motivated to prepare a special place shielded with a partition in a corner of the Linen Room in the basement of the Company Building, where l used to sit and read undisturbed.

I was reading the Bible on one occasion when suddenly l saw a basket like a Baby Cot, linked with a long chain descending from the sky. It was like I was transformed in to my spirit seeing the basket in the sky through the ceiling from the basement of the Company's sixth storey building.

I looked intently for I was curious to know exactly what it was all about. The basket descended right down until I could see the content. I saw a new born Baby in the basket. Then out of my spirit I asked the question "WHAT ABOUT THIS BABY "Then a voice answered and said, "YOU WILL HAVE A BABY BOY IN YOUR OLD AGE AND HIS NAME SHALL BE SAMUEL."

Then immediately the Basket began to ascend in to the sky till it disappeared completely. I was stunned and perplexed as I gave thought to what I had seen and heard; for I had no wife and it was not my intention to get married again for the reason of my bitter experience in marriage.

However, the more I read the Bible the more the Word of God had great impact upon my life. All the bad things I used to do, I did them no more. I found myself changed completely, and the peace of God which passes all understanding now filled my life. It was just like a miracle; I didn't have the desire for women anymore, instead JESUS became my only lover. IT WAS A GREAT TURNING POINT IN MY LIFE.

I started going to Church, and my friend DR. Phillip, a senior Pastor at Kings Temple, encouraged me a lot in my new faith. He introduced a Bible College to me and I enrolled as a Student in 1991. I studied two years at the Salvation Bible College of which DR. Phillip PhD. was the Principal.

I was a very happy man in my new found life in Christ Jesus, and all went well with me. I felt transformed in to a brand new life, serving and worshiping the Lord at Holy Spirit Church in East London. I was also pursuing my Bible Studies vigorously at the SALVATION BIBLE COLLEGE. All the bad and naughty things I used to do I did them no more. I had put all behind me the bad life I used to live.

Thus my spiritual journey with Jesus had started from this time onwards. I continued reading the Bible unabated and the more I read the more the word of God became life to me.

38

A FATAL ACCIDENT AT WORK

Then out blues I had a fatal accident of head injury at work one morning. A renovation work was in progress at the Linen Room, when a new fire door fell on me, and slammed my head on the floor. I was rushed to the Hospital unconscious for many hours and was admitted for months.

Consequently, I was given a sick leave for one and a half years for convalescing. The Word of God says in 1 Thessalonians 5 .18 (In everything give thanks for this is the will of God in Christ Jesus for you.) I realised later on that God allowed it to happen so that I would be available for His purpose.

39

TIME FOR EVANGELISM

Those days gave me more opportunity to serve the LORD by way of evangelism. I started evangelising with Christian Tracts I had prepared myself, and some tracts ordered from America and Australia, visiting every home from Lime House through Canning Town and Popular down to Forest Gate in Newham for almost two years.

I also had time and opportunity to learn the Word of God at the Bible College. Besides I had enough time not only to pray at home but also I visited a number of Prayer Camps in the country of which Ashburnham Prayer Camp was my favourite spot for prayer. I was truly on fire for CHRIST.

40

PRAYER AGAINST ANCESTRAL CURSE IN THE FAMILY

I was in Britain when my Mum sadly passed away in 1981. There was no more death in the family for a long time after her death. Then some years later my senior brother died followed by my elder sister and then another sister also passed away soon afterwards.

About six months later my junior brother took ill for a while and he also died. The death toll of my family members in a short period of time gave me too much to bear, and I set out to fast and pray.

As I continued praying, news reached me saying my eldest nephew had died, and that his junior brother was also seriously ill. It was also revealed that all the family members had died from similar protracted illness. I became so disturbed in my spirit, and I went away to a prayer camp to seek the face of the Lord. The Lord had pity on me and I received a revelation by the Holy Spirit that the cause of death upon my family was due to a "generational curse." The older generation of my family had already been wiped out by the curse. Then I set out to pray day and night on the Word of God, James 5: 15, to break the curse that was upon my family. I cried as I prayed for God's favour and His forgiveness upon our family in the name of Jesus Christ.

God being faithful, He heard and answered my prayer and the death toll in my family stopped.

My junior nephew who fell victim to the curse did not die till I returned to Ghana after some years later. I believed God wanted me to see the condition in which my people died for He had revealed it to me in a dream warning me to stop living in sin.

While in Ghana the information I received revealed that my senior brother had brought an idol in to the family house for the family members to worship. That was the beginning of the family doom. I give God the Almighty, all the glory for His amazing grace and His unfailing love for me. I live today because of His great love and His unfailing grace.

Romans 8:38-39. "For I am persuaded that neither death nor life, nor angels nor principalities nor powers, nor things present nor things to come, 39) nor height nor depth, nor any other created thing, shall be able to separate us from the love of God which is in Christ Jesus our Lord."

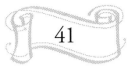

41

REDUNDACY IN 1992

Nearly two years after the incident of my head injury, I was still at home convalescing, when I received a letter from my employers, The INTERNATIONAL HOTEL ORGANISATION, announcing voluntary redundancy for all interested staff. I decided to seize the opportunity as I needed more time to recover from my head injury and to regain my failing memory before I could do any hard work. It was also a decision to help solve my financial needs. So therefore I applied for a voluntary redundancy in 1992.

The decision also gave me more opportunity to be involved in the things of God. From this time onwards I worshipped and served the Lord with all my heart, and with all my soul. I was baptised and groomed by the Holy Spirit and my new life in JESUS blossomed.

I found inner peace and joy in my new found life as a Christian. More so being a Pastor gave me the opportunity to attend almost every Christian meeting in London and the End of year Ministerial Conferences. I made more Christian friends as a result, out of which many of them were Pastors. All my many Pastor friends in those days, used to invite me to their meetings and annual conferences.

42

DIVINE ENCOUNTER (THE HOLY SPIRIT TOUCHED ME)

One Friday after midnight I had encounter with the Lord while sleeping in my bed. On that blessed day I retired to bed after fervent prayer in the midnight. While I was deep asleep, I was lifted up from bed and slammed on the floor.

When my eyes opened, I was lying on the floor singing and weeping but with joy. The song I was singing was a new song, but I continued singing and weeping all the time nonstop, till daybreak. It was very strange, but I could not strain myself from weeping.

Tears flow when I thought about the love of God as I sang, then some unspeakable joy bubbled from within and came out with joyful tears. As the day advanced on that Blessed Friday, I continued singing songs of Praise and worshiping the Lord with joyful tears in the closet of my Home. The singing of Praises and Worship songs gave me appetite and therefore food was no object to me. I fasted all day on that blessed Friday as I remained in doors, singing and worshiping the Lord with joyful tears.

This episode of singing and weeping did not leave me for many days and years; even as at now when Praise and Worship songs are being sang in the Church, my tears flow; tears of joy as I meditate about the grace and the love of God.

That blessed Friday was a great day in my entire life, ---THE DAY THE LORD TOUCHED ME---- I have since then declared every Friday as a day of fasting in my Christian life.

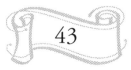

My Graduation From Bible College, Then The Appointment And Inauguration Of My Apostleship As A Pastor.

Meanwhile in exactly two years hence, I graduated from the Bible College. It was a very great occasion for me, and many members of our congregation attended the Graduation ceremony.

In the following weekend the Church congregation organised a dinner party for me in honour of my graduation. Not long afterwards my Spiritual Father Bishop GRAHAM officially inaugurated me as an Associate Pastor in addition to other three Associate Pastors for the HOLY SPIRIT CHURCH with a congregation of about 600 members.

I served the Lord as an Associate Pastor at H.S.C for two years, and I had the conviction to serve at a new founded Church, Revival Pentecostal Church as a Pastor. The R.P.C. Leadership had invited me to help; and after taking it to prayer, I asked my Spiritual Father to allow me to leave. I served at the R.P.C. from the year 1996.

44

SERVING AT REVIVAL
PENTECOSTAL CHURCH

I took over the Evangelical Ministry and went round the whole Community with my team, evangelising with Christian tracks I had prepared, going from house to house for souls. The Lord was with us as He gave us favour and the Church grew considerably and I was very happy indeed. At the same time there were some little quibbles and infighting among the Leadership.

Suddenly the Church leaders called for an emergency meeting. When I attended the meeting the two fellow Pastors angrily demanded that my name should be removed from the Christian Tracts that I had prepared for the Church Evangelism.

We were three Pastors invited by the Leadership to help the Ministry. My fellow Pastors thought I needed favour for the position of the senior Pastor, yet to be appointed by the Leadership, but I had not even thought about it and they accused me in the wrong which made me so sad. I went home and cried bitterly unto the Lord in front of my altar.

Few days later I felt going away and wait upon the LORD and pray. Therefore I said good bye to the Elders of the Church and went away to ASHBURNAM Prayer Camp. I was away for about one week praying and seeking the face of the Lord.

While there I had a dream and that was a clear revelation concerning the Church. I dreamed and there was a big commotion and infighting that had erupted in the Church during my absence.

When I returned to London from ASHBURNAM, some members of the Congregation phoned to tell me all about the serious argument and confusion that had erupted in the Church during my absence; and that the two Pastors have resigned and gone away. I realised that the Lord we serve is awesome and ever faithful.

The next Sunday saw me at the Church Service, and the Elders told me all that had happened while I was away. Everything they told me was exactly what I saw in the dream. That day I believed in the Lord the more, and I realised that our God we serve is an awesome GOD.

However, I was so much disturbed in my spirit, and I went home to pray concerning everything that was happening in the Church, and I asked the LORD for direction.

SERVING AT CHRISTIAN
FAITH MINISTRY

Few days later a Christian friend asked me to lead her to a place to see a friend. We went into a house at West Ham where I met a Man of God who is a Pastor of a Church. He asked me a few questions and when he got to know that I was a Pastor, he asked if I would like to work with him. I told him that I would pray concerning his request.

So I did and I believed, it was the will of God for me to work with him at the CHRISTIAN FAITH MINISTRY. In 1998. I served at the Ministry until the day, I WENT BACK HOME TO FULFILL GOD'S MISSION in 2000.

I RECEIVED PROPHECY IN 1995---- I HEARD HIS VOICE

One day in 1995, before graduating from the Bible College, I was praying in my closet after midnight when I heard a still voice of the LORD saying, (YOU WILL RETURN TO YOUR COUNTRY WITH THE GOSPEL FOR THE SALVATION OF YOUR PEOPLE IN YOUR HOME TOWN, FOR THEY ARE PERISHING).—

Before this time I was wondering how God possibly spoke audibly to His people in such encounter. "Now I know", I said to myself; but the message I received was not very clear to me, and it was not what I expected; for I had decided not to go back to Ghana my country anymore as it was not possible for me to travel outside the country without resident permit or approved Passport. Besides I had not enough savings for my journey back home. Thirdly my dear Mum had expired and there was no reason for me to go back home. I meditated upon all these things for some time and I forgot about it all.

However, I went on with my Christian life as never before, serving and worshipping the Lord. CHRIST WAS THE ONLY LOVER OF MY SOUL IN THOSE DAYS.

PART SEVEN

47

MISSION TO LONDON
AND IT`S IMPACT

One notable Christian gathering was the MISSION TO LONDON. It was one such International Christian Evangelical meeting, organised by Morris CERULLO, an International Evangelist. The Crusade was organised to take place in London every year.

He mobilised many great men of God, Teachers, Pastors, Prophets, Apostles, Evangelists, and great Gospel Singers from big Churches around the World to attend the great Crusade. They came in their splendour to teach, to preach, to testify, to prophesy, and to bless all the masses of the great crowd of Christians and non-Christians alike who were gathered at the Kensington big Stadium.

He also invited as many Pastors as he could get from almost every Church in London to be part of the big Crusade. The Pastors were organised to get together to pray fervently an hour earlier before each section of the meeting started. Similar crusades were organised in the capitals of many countries around the world to seek as many as lost souls for Christ.

In 1994, the MTL executives organised the School of the HOLY SPIRIT for all the Pastors and all Christians alike to learn more about the Holy Spirit, who He is and His functions in the Old and the New Testament. One of the notable Lecturers was Benny HINN. Those who could go through the full Course were presented with Certificates of the Holy Spirit, and I was one of the recipients.

PRAYER FOR ALL THE NATIONS --- HOME CELL PRAYER GROUP.

Morris CERULLO who was also recognised as God's Prophet, encouraged as many as one million Pastors around the GLOBE as it was officially announced to organise Home Cells prayer groups to pray for the salvation of many lost souls around the world. Indeed I counted myself blessed to be one of the chosen Pastors.

My prayer group was based at Stratford in Sister Jane's home at St. Peter's Road. I was given a list of prayer topics for my group by the MTL Executive; and this gave us a guide line as what urgent issues to pray about daily for the year. We used to meet every Friday night and prayed till day break. We continued this prayer assignment for many years until the day I left the Country to go back home on a Mission.

I was presented with a Silver Plated Barge as a Master Sergeant of God's Army; and also a Holy Spirit inscribed "Tie Pin" as a special award by the MTL Executive. My prayer group prayed fervently all those years, and the Lord was favourable with us, and miracles took place in those days.

49

A WOMAN HEALED OF BREAST CANCER

One of my prayer partners, Sister Jane knew of a woman called Nana who had a breast cancer. Jane asked me to go with her to Nana's home to pray for her. When we went to Sister Nana's house, her husband was not happy for our presence, but we prayed for her anyway. We went back to pray a couple of times for Nana against her husband's wish.

In effect therefore we decided to pray for Nana at our prayer meetings, and also I asked my prayer team members to remember Nana always in their prayers at home. I fasted sometimes to pray for her healing from cancer. A few months went by and Sister Jane called me on phone one day screaming in jubilation with the words, "Pastor John, sister Nana is healed! She is healed! She is healed!" Without delay I drove in haste to Sister Jane's house, and sister Nana confirmed that she had been to the Hospital and the Doctor had confirmed there was no cancer present with her anymore. She went back to the Newham Teaching Hospital a few days later and the Specialists confirmed that Nana was free from cancer. There was an unspeakable joy as we gave thanks unto the Lord; and our jubilation was so great as Nana joined our prayer Group.

She also happily joined my Evangelical Team and we gave God all the GLORY, all our thanks and all our praise! I was in those years evangelising with Christian Tracts from door to door throughout Newham Borough. I had by that time finished evangelising with my team from Lime House through Poplar and Canning Town to Forest Gate.

Nana happily devoted all her time for serving the Lord, and she became my Spiritual daughter. She constantly used to call me on phone to pray with her every night before she went to bed. I was so happy for Nana's new life in Christ, and she never did anything on her own without discussing it with me.

50

HIDDEN SECRET OF NANA

But somehow all along, there was a secret in Nana's life which she failed to disclose to me. I did not know exactly what it was, but I had a revelation while praying one day and the Holy Spirit prompted me to ask Nana what she had to reveal to me. Consequently, I summoned Nana to a meeting and when I asked her if she had anything in her life to tell me, she said she had nothing to disclose to me.

However, I consistently enquired with great concern if there was any secret in her life, she would share with me, in accordance with the revelation I had received by the Holy Spirit but she still insisted there was nothing to tell me about.

The Bible says in – (Jeremiah 17:9- The heart is deceitful above all things, And desperately wicked; who can know it.) Some months passed by and Nana developed some pain in her breast, but she felt reluctant to tell me about her pain.

However I got to know about it later. She went to the hospital to find out and the Doctor told her she had developed cancer in her breast. All the members of the Prayer Group were shattered, but I assured them that our God could do it again, therefore they should not be afraid. Few months later, Nana decided to travel to Ghana to see her family.

While she was away I had a revelation again that Nana was hiding something in her life and she needed to confess. 1John 1.9 'If we confess our sins, He is faithful and just to forgive us our sins and cleanse us from all unrighteousness'.

When she returned from Ghana I made all efforts to find out what it was that she had to confess, but she would not tell me. This time her breast cancer was growing from bad to worse. I called all the Church Congregation together to start a corporate prayer for Nana. We continued praying unabated but with little progress.

Few weeks later the Lord revealed in a dream to a sister in our Church congregation, saying she went to Nana's house in the dream and she found something hiding under her bed and so she should tell me to find out what she was hiding.

In effect, I went to Nana after Church service and enquired of her as according to the revelation of our sister's dream, but Nana denied and said she had nothing to hide. Then I said to her it has got nothing to do with me but with the LORD; and that she could not lie to the Holy Spirit.

51

DISOBEDIENCE
---- GOD HATES.

I was so concerned about Nana when I realised that our sister's dream has confirmed all that the Lord had revealed to me. This time Nana was growing weaker and weaker but she would not humble herself for the Lord to come in.

I invited four Pastors to join me one Sunday to pray for Nana, but before we started praying, I had to ask her again if there was any confession she would like to make, but her answer was still negative. The Bible says in (Acts: 5. 3} "Ananias why has Satan filled your heart to lie to the HOLY SPIRIT........? The following week Sunday morning, Nana phoned and asked me to see her urgently, "please come immediately," she added. I was ready for Church Service and I passed through to see Nana. When I got to her house I found her seriously ill; and all the family members had gathered around her sick bed. When she saw me she ordered everyone to leave the room including her husband.

Then she said, she had something to tell me. When I asked what it was, she confessed, and said she had been having an affair with another man outside her marriage, and that, she was ashamed to tell me when I asked. She added she didn't want to be disgraced before men but would rather prefer to be ashamed before God.

I became so sad the whole day, but before the Church service was over, Nana had been taken to the Hospital. I followed up to the hospital to pray for her after Church service. That very evening I drove to North London Stamford Hill to see a friend, and on my way I received a phone call that Nana had passed away. I was extremely sad, and I wept bitterly. I wept for many reasons which I found it hard to explain, even now. I F E A R E D G O D G R E A T L Y T H E M O R E, S I N C E.

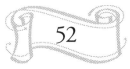

52

GOD'S FAVOUR REVEALED IN THE CROWN COURT

One day I was driving home from a Church meeting when I was involved in a car accident with a cyclist. I had to do a right turning from a major road when a cyclist approaching from opposite direction fell from his bi-cycle as he panicked.

He was not concentrating on the road but rather looking away in to a shop on the road side. Because he was no-where near my car I drove on, but a police patrol car followed up and stopped me a distant away. I tried to explain about the incident to the police but they would have none of it, instead they gave me summons to meet them at the magistrate court. As much as I was disturbed by the incident, I set out to pray for God's favour in this case. When the date of the court hearing was due I attended the Court not knowing exactly what could be the outcome or what my fate would be.

When the case was called the police enthusiastically presented their charges accusing me of reckless and dangerous driving. There were three sitting judges who listened to all the charges attentively as the police presented their case. When that done the senior judge asked me in the dock whether I was guilty or not guilty? I answered, not guilty.

Then suddenly the three judges put their heads together as I was wondering what they were discussing concerning me. After their consultation with each other, the senior judge seated in the middle began to announce, Mr. YEBOAH, he said the court find you not guilty you may go home. My joy was indeed, indescribable. With great jubilation, I rushed out from the court room praising the Lord with great joy. IT WAS MY GOD WHO DELIVERED ME FROM ALL.

PRAYER CAMP

53

SECOND PROPHECY
RECEIVED AT ASHBURNHAM
PRAYER CAMP

In 1996 I went to wait upon the LORD and pray at Ashburnham Prayer Camp as I used to do all those years. I went away for one week, fasting till 6 pm. daily and praying all night till day break at the Prayer Tower. While praying on my last night I felt the presence of the Holy Spirit all over me at the Prayer Tower.

As I sat still, I heard a still voice saying, "YOU WILL GO BACK TO YOUR COUNTRY GHANA, WITH THE GOSPEL FOR THE SALVATION OF YOUR PEOPLE; FOR THEY ARE PERISHING. YOU WILL BUILD MY CHURCH AT BUNSO YOUR HOME TOWN WHEN YOU GO." This message confirmed the previous message I received in 1995, except that building of the Church was not mentioned at that time. When I heard the message, I summoned the courage and asked. "Lord, how could I build a Church seeing I have not enough money to do so?" The voice answered and said, "DO NOT BE AFRAID, YOUR NEEDS WOULD BE PROVIDED, BUT DO NOT DELAY WHEN THE TIMES COMES." Now the message this time gave me too much to bear, and I set out to meditate about certain hard facts.

If I had to go to Ghana, it would mean I had to leave behind my property and all that I had acquired in Britain with no one taking charge on my behalf. More so with the hard fact that I had no Resident Permit to live in Britain at that time, was evident that if I were to travel outside the country, I could not possibly come back.

However, in the face of all these obstacles, I trusted the Lord, put all behind me and continued praying as usual.

54

SELLING CHRISTIAN BOOKS & LITERATURE AS PART OF MY EVANGELISM

As narrated in the previous chapter I took up evangelism as my desire to win souls for Christ. In support of the Evangelical ministry, I decided to sell Christian books and literature at every Christian gatherings or meetings I attended.

Eventually I decided to open a Christian Book Shop at the Stratford In-Shop, but I could not acquire a space in the end. I therefore ended up working at Newham Christian bookshop in East London. I worked voluntarily without pay in the Christian Bookshop in support of my Evangelical Ministry.

I served in the Shop for nearly two years, and as faithful as I worked in the Bookshop, the Proprietors left the Shop under my care, as they moved to live in the country side. I managed the shop on my own for about nine months and it was finally closed down for good.

55

SALE OF MY PROPERTY

In the year 1998 I put my property out for sale, and it remained on the market for a while before it was sold in 1999. The equity on the sale of the House was very good and that happened to prove how faithful our God is.

I was fully convinced that the Lord had a plan for me to go to Ghana on my assignment at this period of time as He had commanded. I was also delighted to note, I had enough provision for my journey as He had promised. One thing significant was that the amount of cash I thought I would need for my journey which I prayed for was miraculously received. My God is always good, awesome and ever faithful.

56

PROPHECY OF BABY
BOY FULFILLED

IT was more than ten years since I had a divorce from my former wife, and it had never crossed my mind to get a new wife. Indeed I had decided not to get married any more for the reason of the bitter experience I had in my previous marriage. Besides Jesus was the only lover of my soul and I did not want to be engaged in any other relationship.

However my Christian friends as well as my Spiritual father Bishop Graham now in America, consistently advised against being single as a man of God.

In effect I set out to pray concerning one sister Judy in the Church and I enquired of Bishop Graham concerning her. Bishop approved of Judy and I made up my mind to marry her because I loved her. I therefore informed Pastor Samson a great man of God who put us through counselling for three months. We got married in 1999, and I loved Judy very much.

The marriage ceremony was officiated by Pastor Samson a man of God with other twelve Pastors in attendance. Also in attendance were all the members of our Church congregation who were present to make the occasion a success. SO JUDY AND I GOT MARRIED AND

SAMUEL THE PROMISED SON WAS CONCEIVED AND BORN IN THE YEAR 2000, TEN YEARS AFTER THE PROPHECY.

As married couples I needed to share with my wife all about my spiritual life and my entire encounter with the Lord. I told her how I received the prophecy about Baby Samuel, and also the revelation concerning His commandment for me to go back to Ghana to build a ministry for the salvation of my people. Also I discussed the time frame of the Lord's plan for me to return to Ghana with the Mission. So therefore the promised son SAMUEL was born in November 2000.

PART EIGHT

57

THE APPOINTED YEAR
FOR HIS MISSION.

The year 2000 was to me a year of vision. I knew in my spirit without doubt that this was the appointed year of the Lord for my journey back home to fulfil His mission. John 20:21- So Jesus said to them again, "PEACE TO YOU! AS THE FATHER HAS SENT ME, I ALSO SEND YOU." So the Lord sent me. One thing significant was that the amount of money required for my journey which I prayed for was divinely provided, and that was a miracle.

Having had the entire requirement needed for my journey back to Ghana, I bid my Church congregation farewell and presented to each of them a Bible, signifying the Word of God with love. The Church also presented to me a Computerized Bible, signifying their appreciation for my service.

When the appointed time of the Lord came I bought my flight ticket and bid my wife Judy and baby Samuel farewell, and they saw me off at the Heathrow Airport.

((John 20:21 so Jesus said to them again, "Peace to you!
As the Father has sent Me, I also send you."))

58

A Journey Back Home On A Mission. (The Return) From London To Ghana.

My journey back to Ghana from London after 24 years stay in Britain was the result of the prophecy I received in my closet in 1995, and then at the Ashburnham Prayer Centre in the year 1996. The journey took me six hours flight from Heathrow Airport to Kotoka International Airport, Accra.

At the Airport to meet me was a relative Sophia, popularly known as Sophie, who received me in to her home. I arrived in Accra at night and at day break I found myself in a different environment. As time went by I realized, I was completely a stranger in my own country. The popular places I used to know were no more the same, and indeed the Accra city as a whole had been transformed completely. I stayed in Accra for a couple of months with an idea of looking for a plot of land for development, but it was not easy to come by.

59

MY JOURNEY TO BUNSO (BACK HOME WITH A MISSION)

Without much progress, I decided to go to Bunso my home town to meet the family. My visit to Bunso was also the beginning of my Ministry and the start of my Mission.

When I got to Bunso, news of my arrival spread fast and wide throughout the town and many of the town folks, especially the youth, the children and the old rushed to the family house to meet me. There were many family members present to welcome me, but many amongst them I did not know especially the youth, for most of them were born during my absence due to the reason of the time span I had been away.

Besides all that, the crowd was very hilarious and excited to see me and they burst in to singing songs of praise and songs of thanksgiving unto the Lord. As I joined the singing of praises and thanksgiving, I became very happy in my spirit as the crowd grew. It was so sensational and I felt the Holy Spirit was upon me.

60

REVELATION OF A VISION IN 1984 FULFILLED

I asked them to form a circle around me as we continued singing. I led them in to prayer and as we prayed I remembered a revelation I had in London one day in 1984 at, all- night prayer meeting, organised by one Prophet Jumah from Congo. I did not know this Prophet and I was not keen to even attend the all-night prayer meeting, for lack of interest, but a friend convinced me to.

While praying with others on that day I was transformed in to my spirit and I found myself standing in the centre of my family house surrounded by family members. It was long time ago and I had forgotten all about it, until suddenly I remembered the revelation in a split second as I began to pray with the people who had come along to welcome me. This revelation occurred long time ago in London, but it was fulfilled that very day I arrived at Bunso from Britain.

61

A PROPHECY BY THE PROPHET WAS ALSO FULFILLED.

At the same night prayer meeting in 1984.the Prophet I did not know before, rightly revealed that I had planned to go to my home town in Ghana but if I did I would not return alive. That meant it was advisable for me not to make the journey. But that advice was not acceptable to me; for I was desperate to see my Mum. I found it very difficult to obey the prophecy but in the end I did not make the journey anyway.

Lo and behold, my junior brother who was to meet me at Bunso as planned was there on that day but he could not return to his destination but died after a protracted illness. This prophecy was remembered at the very moment I was surrounded by the people; and also remembered was the death of my junior brother on the very day I arrived.

I lost my brother so painfully and I could not get over it for a long time. However, my God has always been so gracious unto me for sparing my life then and even now. Unto Him and to Him alone be all the Glory!

62

REVELATION OF DREAM IN 1989 FULFILLED AT BUNSO

One more significant revelation fulfilled was the very day I saw my nephew Fiifi lying in his sick bed with a "bony skeleton" body, lean and fragile. Immediately I saw him, I remembered a dream I had somewhere in1992 as recorded in the previous chapter of this book.

In the dream I saw a really sick man with a "bony skeleton" figure just like a sick dog standing under canopy of a tree. As I walked closer I realised that the sick person I was seeing was me, myself. When I saw that I shook violently with fright in bed and my eyes opened.

I was trembling and shivering in bed when suddenly I heard a voice saying, "unless you changed from your bad life you will surely be like him". That very day I made a decision to quit my bad life behaviour, and I stopped living an immoral life for good.

In fact I feared God greatly since then, and I decided to live a changed life. I have no desire for women anymore. Jesus was my only lover. This was how I lived my life those years after my encounter with the Lord, until I returned home to Bunso, and all the years I spent over there fulfilling His mission.

The very day I entered our family home and saw my nephew in that deplorable condition lying on that bed, then suddenly I remembered the dream I had in 1992. Surely I knew that the God we serve is true and ever faithful.

I believed the Lord wanted my nephew to live for me to see how my people perished under the curse, just as He revealed to me in the dream. I would have been in the same situation if I had not been obedient to the word of God.

63

A GENERATION OF MY FAMILY WIPED OUT

One worrying thing I observed was that one complete older generation of my family members had been "wiped out," passed away; leaving only the younger generation.

My Mum had thirteen children and all have passed away, except myself, my senior sister and our last born. The informers had it that all the family members who were affected under the curse died in the same shameful condition in which I found my nephew Fiifi when I arrived. Had it not been His amazing Grace and His unfailing love, I would have been one of the victims of the venom of the generational curse that gripped our family.

That was exactly what the Lord revealed to me in the dream and warned against the bad way of life I used to live.

64

MY VERY EARLY DAYS MINISTRY WITH MY SISTER IN MY HOME TOWN REMEMBERED.

One time I was meditating very hard about the Grace and mercy of God upon me and how the Lord has graciously spared my life and that of my sister from the generational curse which fell upon our family, when suddenly I remembered our early days Ministry.

When I was a kid about ten years old, a man called Yaw Osei brought an idol called Tigare from the north of Ghana into the town. The Tigare shrine was installed in his house and it had the power to catch the witch crafts in the night and exposed them in the day time through their own self confession.

Those who refused to make self- confession were killed. In effect many town folks submitted themselves to worshipping the idol, but my senior sister called Felicia took to the street to preach the gospel of Jesus and denounced the idol as a false god. She asked me to join her mainly to sing the gospel songs with her in the course of her preaching.

We consistently preached the gospel daily in the street and invited the people to accept JESUS instead of the false god. As we continued to denounce the Tigare as a false god, people feared that the god Tigare could apprehend us and destroy us or kill us, but that could not and did not happen.

When I returned home from abroad to see my sister alive and that she had survived the generational curse, it reminded me of our early day's faith and ministry. Indeed our God is faithful and compassionate towards His children who put their trust in Him.

He has indeed given us power through Jesus Christ to overcome the curse of the law as according to Romans 6:14. –'For sin shall not have dominion over you for you are not under the law but under grace.' Glory be to His Holy name for His abounding grace.

My Ministry Has Begun

That day I arrived at my family house as already recorded, we continued singing songs of praises, worshiping the Lord, and as we did, many people came and filled the house to capacity.

I began to share the word of God, how Jesus is good and how He loves us all. I prayed with them and when I made an altar call for salvation, six of them accepted Jesus as their personal saviour. My ministry had begun and it was later named the "Living Christ Ministry" after days of prayer.

From that day I began to distribute a box full of translated Bible in our vernacular language to all those who needed one. The Church service was held temporally in my rented house on Sundays, and many souls came to receive JESUS as their personal saviour, until the Church was transferred to the ground floor of the Mission House a year later.

At this time the Church was growing considerably as the Lord gave increase to the ministry. IT WAS DURING THIS TIME WHEN THE CHURCH WAS REGISTERED AT ACCRA REGISTRAR OFFICE AS A CHARITABLE ORGANISATION UNDER THE NAME GOSPEL VISION CHAPEL, Inc. OF LIVING CHRIST MINISTRY,

66

EARLY MIRACLE WITNESSED

I continued praying for my nephew Fiifi, almost every day, and to the surprise of all around, he could by now get up from bed after many years of protracted illness to go to the bath room with a helping hand. He could even come to Sunday Church Service with an assistance. It was amazing, but that was the beginning of what God was about to do in Bunso. 'UNTO GOD BE ALL THE GLORY.'

DAWN PREACHING
COMMENCED

The very day I arrived at Bunso my home town, and in the following morning at 3 AM I took to the streets and began preaching the Gospel through the town till day break at 6 a.m.

This Dawn Preaching, as I called it, continued every day for many months and then every other day for about one year unabated, for I was on fire for Christ. A few members of the new Congregation joined me to take the Gospel to the streets and indeed God showed Himself strong as many miracles happened. In the course of the preaching we also went in to some homes to pray for the sick.

PART NINE

68

LAND FOR THE MINISTRY PROJECT AND THE BUILDING FOUNDATION LAID.

In the next day I went round to greet the elders and the Chief of the town as a sign of respect according to our custom. I discussed with them about the land I needed for my Ministry project, and the Chief was pleased to give me a land about two plots for the building of the Mission House; and his linguist Okyeame Baah also gave me a three acre land which I bought for one million Ghana Cedis for the building of the Church and a Prayer Camp.

The work of the project was started in full swing by a Building Contractor and his team of workers who were engaged from Accra. They did a good job in the first year but in the end they caused a lot of problems.

THE CHURCH BUILDING and THE MISSION HOUSE BUILDING FOUNDATIONS WERE BEAUTIFULLY LAID.

CHURCH BUILDING FOUNDATION

MISSION HOUSE BUILDING FOUNDATION

69

BUILDING MATERIALS STOLEN

The building construction progressed successfully for one and a half years and the foundations of both Mission House for the Ministry, and the Church Temple buildings had been beautifully laid and the building work progressed to the lentil stage. Then a shocking discovery was made.

The Building Contractor nicknamed "foreman", and his workers were caught red handed, stealing the building materials including quantity of bags of cement from the site and sold them in a commercial town a few miles away. They were reported to the police and all of them were arrested but the foreman managed to run away.

The Police pursued him but he sneaked through the net, bolted away and disappeared from the scene completely for months, and I had to engage another Builder to continue the work.

While I was away from town, the foreman came back to attack the builders I had engaged on the work and wounded one of them. He run away and I had not seen him since, until about two years later I received sad news that he had gone insane, and was therefore put in chains and transported from Accra to Kumasi his home town.

It was not quite a year later I received another sad news that the foreman had passed away.

One of the suspects called Ben who also jumped court bail could not be apprehended by the police before I travelled to U.K. When I returned from the United Kingdom I realised that Ben, the suspect who jumped court bail was seriously ill, and had grown very lean. When I saw him outside his house I was shocked and after asking him the cause of his illness, I prayed for him.

Glory be unto the Lord, for by His Grace the boy recovered from his illness in a few weeks' time. In the end I withdrew the case against the boys from the Court eventually; and I forgave them all. BEN AND SOME OF THE BOYS INVOLVED IN THE STEALING CASE ARE NOW MEMBERS OF THE CHURCH; AND BEN'S WIFE IS NOW A LEADER OF THE WOMEN'S FELLOWSHIP. GLORY BE UNTO THE LORD.

70

(MIRACLES) WITCH CRAFT ACTIVITIES REVEALED.

The building of the Mission House had progressed to the first floor flow, and the Church Building had got to the stage of the pillars raised on the foundation platform. Prayers were being offered consistently for the progress of the ministry project and for the growth of the Living Christ Church.

By God's grace the Church had by now moved in to the ground floor apartment of the Mission House. The Dawn Preaching was going on every Tuesday morning un-relented and the Lord was gracious unto us. It was one such Tuesday morning, while the dawn preaching was in progress, a young man called Dickson came walking dizzily following us and trying to disrupt the preaching. He was noted for his drinking habit in town and he looked drunk at the hour of the day.

As he was causing confusion my people threw him out, but he made second attempt to follow us. I advised them not to reject him, but to watch over him. He followed us until day break and when we got home at the Mission House, he slammed his body on the verandas, while we went inside the prayer room to pray and to thank the Lord as we normally used to do.

We came out after prayers to meet him still lying down, his body prostrated on the floor. They woke him up and he told them he wanted to see the Pastor.

When I asked him what it was about, he told me he had something to disclose to me. I took him inside the prayer room, and for a moment a weird revelation started to unfold.

He revealed to me that he was a witch; and he began to tell me all about their witchcraft activities in the night against the Church which had been going on for some time now. He said he had been trying for weeks or months to come to me to confess, but his spiritual partners in crime would not let him; for any time he wanted to join me at the time of dawn preaching, they would slam him down in the spirit and he could not get up from bed.

He went on to tell me that he belonged to a witchcraft kingdom and their king was one Biko. Biko was a distant relation to me, but in real life he was notorious, wretched, a drunkard, and had no aim in life; but in spiritual realm he was a king.

Dickson told me that one major assignment of their group was to dig gold from under the foundation of the temple or the new Church building; and as they dug trenches under the building he would support the foundation with some poles to save it from falling. For that reason his colleagues would seek to punish him, but he would turn a frog and jump in long stripes to flee from them.

The demons' mission was to destroy the foundation of the temple spiritually. He explained that his spiritual symbol as a witch was a long legged frog and that he was always able to flee from any imminent danger.

He told me that he liked me and that's why he had come to confess to me. Proverb 16.7-'When a man's ways please the Lord, He makes even his enemies to be at peace with him.' He added that he would like to work with me in the Church whereby the sick would come for prayer and he would gather leaves from the bush in the night to prepare local concussion or herbs medicine to heal the sick; and when it so happened, it would be a form of miracle by the Church which could induce many to join the Church.

I replied, and said angrily, may God forbid that I would allow your witchcraft activities to be part of God's Church. THE LORD OUR GOD WHO CREATED ALL THINGS, AND WHO SENT ME IS MORE POWERFUL TO DO GREATER MIRACLES IN THE CHURCH, I replied.

I told him, you need salvation, come and we would pray for you; and you would be saved." He did not agree but left and never returned. Biko, supposedly the chief or the king of the witchcraft group has since died when I was on holiday in Britain.

71

LAND – LITIGATION, BETWEEN ME AND CHIKA.

There were so many attacks physically and spiritually which were meant to cause many distractions and disruptions, but in all I was not moved and the Lord's favour gave me victory all through.

Chika was a sister to Okyeame Baah who sold the land for the Church building to me. She was present and so also were all the members of their family when I paid for the three acre land. Before the site plan could be completed and signed by Okyeame Baah he passed away.

Not quite long afterwards Chika decided to take advantage of her brother's absence and the unsigned document of the site plan, to deprive me of the ownership of the land. She persisted claiming the land from me almost on daily basis as she kept coming to my house.

One morning I saw her a distance away coming, followed by a group of people, so I waited for her outside the house; and before she could say anything I told her to go away from my sight in an angry mood, and seeing that I was very angry, she left with her people quietly. She was noted for her trouble making attitude and she would never stop harassing me, so I took it to prayer. The Lord gave me direction to go and pray on the land on daily basis which I did, and by His grace she has been silent and had never come back unto this day.

72

CONFESSION OF WITCH CRAFT ACTIVITIES IN THE FAMILY

I had a revelation one night about one of my grand-daughters called Baby; and I decided to find out what it was. I called her the following morning and asked what she had to reveal to me. She said there was nothing to reveal to me but when I insisted, she relented and told me everything concerning her activities in the spiritual world.

She said she was a witch and that she always came to the Mission House every night in search for food but she always returned empty handed, because I was always awake. She revealed that six members of the family were witches and they used to come together to the Mission House in the night in search for spiritual food (meaning human flesh) but they always returned empty handed, because I was always awake anytime they came.

She began to name them and the names of their witchcraft symbols in the form of different animals which gave them power to operate in the night.

At this stage I took a pen and Note Book to take notes as she spoke. She added that her symbol of her witchcraft power was a snake. She continued to reveal about all the people they had killed in the family.

They had done much evil in the family, and also they had destroyed the life of my only nephew alive by removing his heart and the mind in the spiritual realm making him totally disabled.

My nephew is called Dr. Dickson, a lecturer at Accra University. He was educated at the University of Edinburgh in Great Britain and had his Doctorate Degree in Agriculture. He is now left with protracted sickness which had made him totally disabled, even before I returned home from abroad.

I was wondering why my nephew would not believe in prayer, and also his wife would not allow any of his family members to visit him. I could never understand the situation until my grand-daughter Baby had revealed all that had taken place spiritually concerning Dr. Dickson.

She narrated that my late senior sister who was also a witch while she was alive sold, Dickson's soul to his wife, also a witch, for a piece of new cloth in spiritual realm. She said his wife had put the sickness on him so that she could collect all Dickson's salary. Therefore she sought help from the family to destroy him.

When I asked why they helped his wife to destroy him she explained that her uncle Dickson did not help her to go to school. Before then I had made several attempts to take my nephew to a prayer camp for intercessory prayer but his wife would not let me and Baffour himself would not like to go; for the wife had threaten him not to go with me. When I insisted, the wife picked up a quarrel with me and told me that even if Dickson died she would bury him herself without telling me.

However, while in London on a holiday in September 2014, I received a message that Dr. Dickson's wife had expired. The evil that men do lives after them.

73
DEMON SPIRIT CAST OUT

Matthew 17: 18, 'And Jesus rebuked the demon, and it came out of him'.
After interrogating Baby, and in the face of all the confessions, she had
made, I asked her if she would like the demon spirit in her to be cast out.
She replied, 'Yes'. As a result I set out to pray concerning Baby's deliverance
and the deliverance of the entire family.

The Holy Spirit led me to the neighbouring town to look for a Man of
God, concerning this matter. When I met him he told me his name was
Elder Johnson, and said he was expecting me because he had a dream about
me even though he had not met me before. From that very hour we began to
pray together a prayer of agreement concerning this matter and the Church.
He came to me the following morning and we continued to pray on the open
land behind the Church building. I summoned Baby to be present at the
prayer meeting and when she was prayed for she fell on the floor, and as I
commanded the demon to come out of her in Jesus name, she vomited. When
she got up eventually she admitted that she felt delivered because the snake
symbolising the evil spirit inside of her had been vomited out. LUKE 9:1
"THEN HE CALLED HIS TWELVE DECIPLES TOGETHER AND
GAVE THEM POWER AND AUTHORITY OVER ALL DEMONS,
AND TO CURE DISEASES"

Then she volunteered to lead me to the location where her witchcraft pot was hidden behind the family house. The pot was full of concoction with blood mixed with water and it was burnt instantly in a flame of fire on the very day.

From there on Baby was set free from the evil bondage, and she became useful in the Ministry as children's teacher. I was so happy about her life transformation and I gave her a new name as Mary Magdalene. I gave the Lord all the Glory for our God is good and He is ever faithful.

74

A MAN WHO ROSE AGAINST ME WENT BLIND.

When I arrived in my home town from Britain, some individuals in town rose against me for no apparent reason at all. Amongst those who hated me most was a man by name Judas. He was one of the elders at the Chief's palace, who opposed anything I did in the town which needed approval by the council of elders.

Eventually something unexpected happened, when it was reported to me that Judas, the enemy had collaborated with a relative of mine to sell out about 10 acres of my farm land for 17 Million Ghana Cedis. The matter was reported to the Police and the leader of the gangsters run away into the neighbouring country. Not quite long a message was received some months later that he had died in a foreign land.

Before Judas could be arrested he made haste to see me with some elders with an apology to forgive him for what he had done. When I told him that he should be punished for the crime he had committed, he broke down and wept bitterly asking for forgiveness. I had pity on him and I forgave him all.

Not many years went by and I had to travel outside the country; and when I returned a year later I was informed by a Good Samaritan that Judas with whom I shared a common boundary of farm land had stolen and cultivated about six acres of my land for Cocoa plantation.

When I asked him about it, he became angry and insulted me; and as a result I summoned him to the Chief. The case could not be called for settlement for some time, because some of the witnesses were not around to testify.

It was time for me to travel outside the country to Britain, and when I returned a year later I was told that Judas the thief had gone blind. The Word of God says concerning His children in Isaiah 41.10 "Fear not for I am with you...........11" Behold all those who were incensed against you"; shall be ashamed and disgraced. They shall be as nothing. And those who strive with you shall perish." To the Lord my God be all the GLORY for putting my enemies under my feet.

75

TOBIA AND SAMBALAT WERE ON ATTACK

The Temple was built to the roofing stage when the Town Committee comprising about Ten Town folks came to the building site early in the morning at dawn, to claim a portion of my land for the Local School which share a boundary with me.

They came there at dawn with the intention of moving or shifting the boundary during my absence. But before they came I was already in the uncompleted Church Building praying, for this is what I used to do every morning for the past year, in accordance to the direction received from the Holy Spirit about a year ago, to continue praying on the land. The attackers were shocked when they saw me around that hour of the day.

They were led by Tomas and Jessie, nick-named, Tobiah and Sanballat –"Nehemiah 4: 7." Their reason being, according to Tobia and Sanballat that I had taken part of the Local school land and they had come to take it from me. I confronted them with the truth concerning the boundary and when the other members of the group realised the truth of the matter they apologised and went away in diverse ways with shame.

Nehemiah 4: 14 ....".Do not be afraid of them. Remember the Lord great and awesome;" -- will fight for you........

I started glorifying the Lord for fighting my battle for me. Isaiah 59.19 'When the enemy comes in like a flood the Spirit of the Lord will lift up a standard against him.' Also the word of God says the enemy will attack in one way but they will flee in several ways. Tomas and Jessie, like Tobia and Sambalat who came with their supporters in a group, left the Church compound in diverse ways drowned in shame. Our God is awesome, and He had never forsaken me in times of trouble but gives me victory always. 2 Chronicle. 20:15 '...Fear not for the battle is not yours, it is mine'. Our God is ever faithful. May His name be glorified!

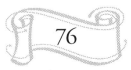

76

THE CHURCH'S COMMITMENT TOWARDS WIDOWS AND ORPHANS AND THE CHURCH - GROWTH ---

The Church had increased considerably and as it's recorded in the previous chapter, we had this time moved in to the ground floor apartment of the Mission House. I made it a policy of the Church to show love for all the widows and the orphans in the town and to organise a party for them and the poor alike at the Mission House on every Christmas Day.

As much as the people and all the widows showed great appreciation for our love towards them, the Lord was gracious unto us and He continued to increase the Church as many miracles happened. On every Christmas Eve, invitations would be sent to all the widows in town to meet at the Mission House for celebration, as we shared a word of God's love. We would also dance to the tune of praise and worship music all night of the Christmas Eve.

The widows would each receive a gift of parcel and some cash for a Christmas dinner. They would also have soft drinks and snacks for the night. Also on Christmas Day, a dinner party would be organised for the orphans and the children from the poor homes. The women as well as the children would go home fulfilled with joy and gratitude. MAY THE NAME OF THE LORD BE GLORIFIED!

A WOMAN BITTEN BY A SNAKE.

One day a woman was bitten by a snake in the farm and she was rushed to the Mission House to be prayed for, before she was sent to the hospital about eight miles away. After she was prayed for, and having given her the necessary first aid, I had to provide transportation for her to be sent to the hospital a distance away from the town. The driver took her to the hospital as we continued praying, and after some time before nightfall, she was brought back from the hospital completely healed. Glory be to God for He is the healer.

78

A Young - Girl Sick Of High Fever Healed

One evening a small girl was rushed to the Mission House seriously ill at the point of death. The mother and the family were crying when they brought her in, and I asked them not to cry, for Jesus was able to heal her. The grand- mother suddenly responded and said, "If she is healed from her sickness then I would come to join the church."

I began to pray for the child in agreement with my church elders who were present at the time. Thank God the child was revived by the power of the Holy Spirit, and I asked the parents to send her home. In the same evening I followed up to visit her with one of my elders and prayed for her before bed time. I went to see her again in the following morning with the Elder to find the small girl completely healed. We greatly rejoiced and praised the Lord for what He had done. To God be all the glory!

79

A Fetish Woman Offered To Do Miracles In The Church.

One day a strange woman, I had never met before, approached me at the Mission House and said she had come to congratulate me for the good work I was doing for the town. She continued to say that she had something important to discuss with me.

When I asked what it was, she began to introduce herself by saying, many people in town knew that she had power to heal the sick and that she could do some miracles for the Church to grow immensely, and we could see great increase as a result. How could this be I asked?

She said if I could fetch her two life frogs she would bury them alive with some mixed concoctions at the two entrances of the Mission House, and we could see an immense growth in the Church.

When I heard that I was filled with holy indignation then I shouted aloud with anger, "the devil is a liar". I turned round to face her, eye ball to eye ball fuming with anger and said, "woman, my God who sent me was able to increase the Church to capacity. May God forbid that such a thing you suggested could happen in this Church! May God forbid?" I exclaimed loudly.

I said to her please leave the house for I do not need your help. She left the scene embarrassed and deeply ashamed. The devil is cunning and truly a liar.

80

ANOTHER BIG TRIBULATION

Since the Ministry project started I had encountered many trials and tribulations, but the worst of all was when the woman I called daughter Sophia wickedly duped me for an amount of twenty one thousand seven hundred pounds. It was the worst tribulation I had ever encountered since the beginning of the project.

She made me totally bankrupt. She cleverly deceived me to give her the money £21,700 (Twenty one Thousand Seven Hundred Pounds) for taking delivery of her goods from the harbour. She took the money from me on two occasions- She borrowed £10,000 on the first occasion, and then £10,000 on the second occasion plus £1,700 given her for safe-keeping. She promised to pay the money back any time I would ask for it. She was rich and wealthy, a very successful business woman and therefore I trusted, she could refund the money she borrowed, at any time I needed it, therefore I decided to help her.

However, I forewarned her that the money was the Lord's, and it was meant for the Ministry project and therefore it should be refunded when needed. She promised to refund the money on each occasion she borrowed from me, as the source of the money was explained to her.

Four months later I phoned to tell her that I needed the money to continue the project, but she shockingly replied- what money? Before I could say anything she continued and said she had nothing to give me. What do you mean? I asked but she didn't respond?

From that moment, I began to shiver as I smelt a wolf in sheep skin. I sensed immediately that she was not prepared to pay back the money. I also knew there and then that it was her concocted plan to dupe me.

When we met to discuss the matter she was angry and even wanted to use her hands on me. She said to me, if I could not continue the project I should better pack it up. She added that she had never come across any single person building a Church and ministry project on his own.

I nearly wept when I realised that she conned me and therefore she was not prepared to pay back the money. I approached her Pastor of Christ Apostolic Church and asked if he could intervene on my behalf, which he did but ended in a heated argument so she quit the Church. That time I had nothing on me and it looked like it was all over; but it was not over until God says it's over.

When I had the opportunity to travel to London, I was compelled to approach GOD TV., for some help but I received no response. I just trusted in the Lord, and how God gave me the strength to continue the Ministry project was another miracle. The project is almost completed as at now by His Grace. Now Sophie's business mansion has collapsed in just six months later, and all her wealth has gone in to the drain. The most-richest woman in Accra big Market Kantamanto popularly known as Anti Sophie is now as poor as a church mouse. However, I have forgiven her all.

PART 10

81

SECOND PHASE OF THE PROJECT

The first phase of the project was completed to the gable stage of the Mission House building; and the Church building as well.

The next stage was the roofing of both buildings. The timber contractors who were to supply timber for the roofing were somehow dishonest; and it caused much delay and extra cost; it also caused many inconveniences.

The carpenters who did the roofing completed that of the Mission House but it was not satisfactorily done. In effect I had to engage another carpenters to do the roofing of the Church building. The roofing of the Church building was nearing completion when it caved in after a heavy down pour of rain.

THE SECOND PHASE OF THE PROJECT

(CHURCH BUILDING ROOF CAVED IN)

Everyone in town and all the congregation alike expressed shock and dismay for what had happened but I assured them that my God was in control and therefore they should not panic. I had to find a new timber for the second roofing. Eventually the work was completed at last by God's grace, and all the congregation jubilated. Matthew 16:18 …..Jesus said …….."I will build My Church and the gates of Hades shall not prevail against it."

The Church building doors, and windows have since been fixed; the walls beautifully painted, and inside the Temple well decorated. The Church building now completed, and named "THE LIVING CHRIST TEMPLE" which is now being used for worship by the congregation. We give GOD all the glory for what He has done.

MY CHILDHOOD DREAM
REMEMBERED

When I was a child I used to say to myself, when I grew up I would put up a Church Building on top of Bunso Hill (as it's popularly called) on the road side at Bunso approach; where everyone could see it from every corner of the town. During my childhood it was always my dream to build a Church and I wanted it to be on the top of that hill.

However, when I returned home from abroad and was initially looking for a land to build, I approached the Bunso Hill Land owners but there was no allocation available. I remembered this childhood dream of mine once again when the roofing of the Church building was completed. I believe God's purpose for my life was to build His Church-for the salvation of souls unto Christ.

83

ANOTHER GREAT
MIRACLE IN MY LIFE

THE UK RESIDENT PERMIT WHICH WAS DENIED ME
WHEN IN BRITAIN FOR 24 YEARS, WAS MIRACULOUSLY
SENT TO ME IN GHANA WHILE FULFILLING GOD'S
PURPOSE-- THE MISSION.

As recorded in the previous chapter, I left Britain for Ghana in the
year 2000 without a U.K. Resident Permit. I stayed in Ghana for about
six years fulfilling God's purpose, (BACK HOME WITH A VISION
FOR A MISSION) building the Ministry, and preaching the gospel
for salvation of souls.

Then something miraculous happened concerning my British
immigration papers. The authorities would not sanction my resident
permit while in Britain for the past 24 years until after I had left the
country for six years.

One day while at the Mission House at Bunso, I received a phone
call from Accra asking me to call London for urgent news which I did.
I was given a surprise message by Pastor Kingsley Adu in London that
my Resident Permit documents had been approved; granting me leave
to stay in the United Kingdom indefinitely, and that my approved
Passport was ready waiting for collection at my London address. 'The

word of God says, where the sole of your foot will tread upon, I have given you.' Joshua 1. 3.

That day was a day of jubilation and I sang songs of praise and thanksgiving unto the Lord my God. (Psalm, 40:5; Many, O Lord my God, are your wonderful works which you have done) The word of God says, 'whatever you lose or leave behind for my sake, you will receive back a hundred fold...' Matthew 19:29." And everyone who has left houses or brothers or sisters or father or mother or wife or children or lands, for my name's sake, shall receive a hundredfold, and inherit eternal life." ... THE GOD THAT I SERVE IS EVER FAITHFUL.

84

A FAINTED MAN AT CHURCH SERVICE WAS REVIVED

It was one Sunday morning service when a member of the congregation totally fainted. His head fell backwards with his eyes wide opened with the black eye balls disappeared in their sockets, his teeth clamped together and unable to talk.

This incident happened in the middle of my sermon, and when someone shouted for my attention, I engaged the whole congregation in fervent prayers and for some time the man's head could not be brought back to normal position and he was still unable to talk. At this time my driver had brought the car and they carried him to the hospital, about 18 miles away, but I never ceased praying with the congregation for the Lord to touch him and revive him. While still praying seriously un-abated for about one hour, we saw the car outside through the window coming back with the man. They came out from the car with the man fully recovered, and they entered the Church singing songs of praise unto the Lord. We turned our prayer into singing, praising the Lord, and dancing with jubilation, giving all the Glory unto the Lord. Apparently the news of the incident had got to the town; and the man's relations and many town folks had joined us in the Church jubilation about the man's miraculous recovery.

According to the driver, before they could get to the hospital about five miles away, the man opened his eyes and spoke saying he would like to visit the loo. They helped him to the loo and after he had finished he came out walking as normal unaided; then he said to them " please take me back to the church, I'm fine, I don't need to go to the hospital anymore," he added. Then I knew, the Lord had touched him, while we continued praying, and healed him before he got to the hospital. Psalm 103 says: "Bless the Lord, O my soul. Who forgives all our iniquities? Who heals all our diseases?" The faithfulness of the Lord and His Grace towards us endure forever more. May His Name, and His Name alone be glorified for all the great things He has done.

85

MY FAITH ACTIVATED AT
THE DOCTOR'S SURGERY

In the year 2006, after I had received my Pass Port from Home Office granting me an indefinite leave to remain in Britain, I travelled to U.K. on a holiday. While in U.K. my friend Pastor Kingsley and his wife Sophia received me in to their home at Romford.

Pastor Kingsley is more of a Brother than a friend to me, and I always called him brother and so did he. We did everything together and even shared our secrets together. My brother often complained of ill health and said he had high blood pressure. As a result his doctor had forbidden him not to eat some variety of food; therefore at the dining table he rejected some delicious dishes which I enjoyed to eat most.

My brother was so concerned and would always therefore warn me to refrain from eating such delicacies, but I would turn down his advice always. He feared I may probably end up suffering from the same sickness he detested most which was dragging him down every day.

However I did assure him that high blood pressure was not my portion and therefore it could not get hold on me. Many days went by and we lived together as one family throughout my holidays. However, it happened one day when I took ill, and went to see my family Doctor at the Surgery. He told me to do a blood test and asked me to return the following morning for the result.

In the following morning I received from the Doctor a bomb shell message concerning the blood test. He said I had developed symptoms of high blood pressure, and that I needed urgent treatment. The shocking message received shocking response from me, when I said to the Doctor, I don't think so, I cannot be sick of high blood pressure. What do you mean, he asked? I replied with clarity that high blood pressure has no power over me. I am a child of God I said.

He thought I was out of my mind, but what he didn't know was that, I was divinely activating my faith. He looked at me intently and said to me go home and come back next week for another blood test. I left the clinic praying in my spirit than never before, rebuking, rejecting and denouncing high blood pressure, or any other sickness in my system till I got home in my car.

I kept quiet and never told anyone what had happened at the hospital, but continued praying consistently all day every day till the end of the week. The word of God says in James 5: 15, "And the prayer of faith will save the sick, and the Lord will raise him up." On Monday of the following week I went back to see the Doctor at the clinic, and he ordered me to do another blood test. I was asked to wait at the Reception for the result. When it was ready the Doctor called me and asked what I had done to my body for the past week. I replied, nothing!

Then he said with amazement, your blood pressure is now normal. I said to him it ought to be so for I prayed unto the Lord. My joy was hilarious and I gave glory unto the Lord in my car all the way home. Then I told the family my story what the Lord had done, and they all rejoiced with me.

From there on my brother engaged me in prayers every day until I returned to Ghana from my holidays.

86

MY FAITH IN THE WORD OF GOD RESULTING MY GENERAL GOOD HEALTH.

The Word of God says in Isaiah 53: 5 ...." And by His stripes we are healed." It also says in 1 Peter 2:24 "Who Himself bore our sins, in his own body on the tree, that we, being dead to sins, should live unto righteousness: by whose stripes we were healed." Up to a time in my Christian life, little did I know, or never did I come to terms with the truth that, good health is God's provision for His children.

After my victory over 'high blood pressure' by faith in the word of God; the Holy Spirit gave me insight of the TRUTH that, God's will for His children is to live in good health. The scripture says in John 8: 32 'And you shall know the truth and the truth will make you free.' I have henceforth abided in the truth of God's Word, and it has set me free from all diseases and I have lived with healthy body for more than ten years up till now. GLORY BE TO GOD.

From there on until this day, Doctors in various Hospitals in London have examined me and diagnosed various sicknesses for my body but I have since refused to accept them all in JESUS name.

In 2006, I was diagnosed as a prostate-cancer patient, and was sent to do a biopsy test which was inconvenient and very painful. In few weeks later I was called back to the Hospital to do a second test with the explanation that the result of the previous test was not clear, but I refused. The Urology Specialist with Asian background asked me why, and I told him I did not think I had cancer, it is not for me I added. He asked why I thought so. I replied, because I am a child of God, and Jesus is my saviour and my healer.

It appeared he was not surprised but agreed with me. He allowed me to go without doing the test; but they have not ceased calling me for series of examinations and blood tests unto this day, yet they have found nothing; and I have experienced no pain in my body up till now. I am cancer-free in Jesus Name!

87

BOWEL CANCER TEST
PROVED NAGATIVE.

In the year 2010, I received a Bowel cancer Test Kit from the NHS to complete. When the test was examined at the Hospital, the Specialists told me there was a bowel cancer symptom present in my body, and that I should report at the London Hospital for further examination and treatment. I did not accept it and therefore refused to go to the Hospital.

The Hospital authorities contacted me on phone, and gave me a date to see them at the Hospital, but I could not attend the appointment, because I was going away on a holiday.

When I returned from my holiday I received another Bowel cancer Kit in 2014 to complete which I did. Few months later the NHS sent me the result saying my Bowel is normal; and that I did not need any more tests.

PRAISE THE LORD! The Scripture says in Hosea 4: 6 "My people are destroyed for lack of knowledge,"

NOW COMPLETELY FREE FROM ARTHRITIS

Notwithstanding my Christian life well before 2002, I used to experience bodily pains in my shoulders, my knees and sometimes my back. The pain was so terrible especially in winter that I could not even lift up my hands above my shoulder level; neither could I bend to pick anything from the floor.

This problem was diagnosed by the Doctors as arthritis; but believing right, that my body is the temple of God and no sickness has any right to live in me; and also living right by exercising my body daily has eliminated the pain from my body completely. I am now entirely free from arthritis for some years past in Jesus Name. I give glory to the Lord my God for He is the reason for my healthy body now, and the normal good health I enjoy every day. I live in divine health and walk in victory every day of my life, Hallelujah!

THE MISSION ACCOMPLISHED

THE CHURCH BUILDING WAS COMPLETED WITH THE DOORS, AND BLUE GLASS WINDOWS FITTED; THE FLOOR CEMENTED AND THE WALLS BEAUTIFULLY PAINTED. THE BUILDING WAS CONNECTED WITH LIGHTS, AND THE CONGREGATION HAVE STARTED WORSHIPPING IN THE CHURCH.

THE CHURCH BUILDING IS CALLED "LIVING CHRIST TEMPLE" AND IT IS YET TO BE OFFICIALLY OPENED. THE STOREY BUILDING OF THE MISSION HOUSE IS ALSO COMPLETED, LEAVING THE PLASTERING AND PAINTING OF THE TOP FLOOR WALLS. HOWEVER THE SENIOR PASTOR OF THE CHURCH NOW LIVES IN THE MISSION HOUSE; AND ALSO PRAYER MEETINGS ARE HELD IN THE MISSION HOUSE FROM TIME TO TIME.

PRAISE THE LORD, FOR THE MISSION COULD NOT HAVE BEEN ACCOMPLISHED WITHOUT THE INTERVENTION OF THE LORD IN THE FACE OF ALL ODDS, TRIALS AND TRIBULATIONS WHICH I ENCOUNTERED IN THE COURSE OF THE MISSION PROJECT.

CHURCH

MISSION HOUSE

NO AMOUNT OF HUMAN EFFORT COULD HAVE SEEN ME THROUGH WITHOUT THE POWER OF THE HOLY SPIRIT and the mighty hand of God; FOR I JUDGED HIM FAITHFUL WHO HAD PROMISED; (HEBREW 10:23). "Let us hold fast the confession of our hope without wavering, for He who promised is faithful."

THE PHYSICAL AND SPIRITUAL BATTLES I ENCOUNTED WERE IMMENSE AND NUMEROUS BUT I WAS NOT AFRAID FOR THE LORD MIRACULOUSLY SAW ME THROUGH ALL. HIS NAME AND ONLY HIS NAME BE GLORIFIED. Now that His Mission is accomplished, I believe there is going to be great revival and great awakening for salvation of many souls in Bunso and in the whole Eastern Region, for I believe He who promised, He is also able to fulfil.

I am sure as I believe, the Glory of the LORD will be seen in Bunso and all over the Country of Ghana in JESUS NAME, AMEN!

90

CHURCH CRUSADES AND REVIVAL MEETINGS AT BUNSO.

Revival and Crusade meetings were organised from time to time at the open space in town centre for salvation of souls with a number of invited Pastors in attendance.

There were also other crusade meetings organised in the neighbouring towns to preach the gospel of Jesus Christ for salvation of souls. Sometimes we had a number of souls saved and the sick also received healing. Glory be unto the Lord. Now the Lord is in control and the Church is growing, for it is the Lord who builds His Church and no gates of hades shall prevail against it.

I have since decided to retire in Briton and have therefore handed over the Church to two Pastors who are doing good job. However I have not ceased praying, for I believe the Lord is about to bring forth a great Revival for salvation of great number of souls not only in Bunso, but also in the surrounding towns in the Eastern Region, with great awakening in the whole country, for His GLORY will be seen by all in the land of Ghana. MAY HIS NAME, AND HIS NAME ALONE BE GLORIFIED!!!

91

CONCLUSION

What God has done in my life, I believe He would equally do the same for every believing disciple of Jesus Christ. Not only did I trust in God for the financial need, but also in answer to prayer God gave me wisdom to manage the work of the Ministry project. The result was above expectation for the Lord showed Himself strong as He did many miracles in the process.

I believe whoever has the same desire in all things to do the will of God and put his trust in Him will receive similar result of blessings. The Building project of the Church and the Mission House is completed and many souls have since been saved.

The word of God says in Matthew 16:18 "And I also say to you that you are Peter, and on this rock I will build My Church, and the gates of Hades shall not prevail against it." I can now boldly say that the Ministry project could not have been completed without the mighty Hand of God. Yes Jesus is the bedrock foundation for the Gospel Vision Chapel, of the Living Christ Ministry. Thank God the Ministry is growing as many souls are being saved.

I believe the Church is not for any individual, for JESUS CHRIST IS THE BED ROCK FOUNDATION of the Living Christ Church;

and was built for the Community of the Town and also indeed for the surrounding Towns in the Eastern Region.

I HAVE NOW HANDED OVER THE GOSPEL VISION CHAPEL of LIVING CHRIST MINISTRY TO THE COMMUNITY OF THE TOWN AND THE CONGREGATION OF THE CHURCH WITH TWO PASTORS IN CHARGE.

I HAVE NOW PERMANENTLY SETTLED IN ENGLAND AS I AM ADVANCED IN AGE. THE MINISTRY AND THE CHURCH IS THE LORD'S AND ALL HIS CHILDREN.

MAY HIS NAME AND HIS NAME ALONE BE GLORIFIED! AMEN!

THE AUTOBIOGRAPHY
OF THE AUTHOR

The book 'BACK HOME WITH A VISION FOR A MISSION' is all about the great and awesome miracles the Lord has done in the entire life of the Author. It also shows how God was merciful upon a boy born into a Christian home, in a village, but grew up into a society of city life living in disobedience to God with his sinful behaviour.

He seldom went to Church, but when he did so on one Xmas Eve, he received a prophecy from the man of God. The same message was miraculously received from two different Men of God in different Churches in three consecutive years. Though the prophecy was fulfilled years later when the author migrated to Britain, yet whether consciously or unconsciously, he failed to give God the glory for what He had done in his life and for his life.

He still grew more idle in the things of God and continued living in all sorts of sin. However, his way of life which was in consistent disobedience to God resulted in near destruction of his life by a protracted illness of heart pain. Nevertheless, the God whom he dishonoured by his wicked and sinful character and unrepentant spirit, had not given up on him. He was like a lost sheep for many years of his life, but when the Lord found him He forgave him all.

One day was the turning point in his life when the author found a Bible at work and decided to read it. The Word of God became life as he continued reading unabated. From that day onwards the prodigal son was found, and the Lord began to do great and awesome miracles in his life, which he thought, were necessary to be recorded for all to see, and to read just for His glory, hence the publication of this book – BACK HOME WITH A VISION FOR A MISSION. I ENTREAT YOU TO READ ON.

Printed in the United States
By Bookmasters